VIRTUAL REALITY THERAPY DISCARD

An Innovative Paradigm

Max M. North, Ph.D.
Sarah M. North, M.S.D.
Joseph R. Coble, Ph.D.

FOR REVIEW AND ...

Max M. North

IPI PRESS ● COLORADO SPRINGS

Published by **IPI Press**
2608 N. Cascade Ave.
Colorado Springs, CO 80907
Phone/Fax: 1-800-333-0220
International Fax: 719-630-1427
Email: ijvr@usa.net

ISBN 1-880930-08-0
Library of Congress Catalog Card Number: 96-94811
Manuscript Editors: H. Trussell Pyle and Anne German Wilson
Printing and Binding: Morris Publishing

Warning: This publication is designed to provide accurate information in regard to the subject matter covered. However, the authors and publisher assume no responsibility for errors, omissions, or other inaccuracies in the information or material, or from any use or operation of any methods, products, instructions or ideas contained in the material herein. In addition, it must be noted that this book is not intended as a substitute for the medical advice of physicians.

Trademark notice
CyberEye is trademark of General Reality Company
Data Glove is trademark of VPL
Flock of Birds is trademark of Ascension Technology Corporation
Indigo is trademark of Silicon Graphics Incorporated
InsideTrack and FastTrack are trademarks of Polhemus
ı   Mouse is trademark of Logitech Corporation
         ˌ trademark of Intell Corporation
      ˌon, dVS, dVISE, and Divisor are trademarks of Division Incorporated
    ˌer Glove is trademark of Nintendo Corporation
ˌuperscape is trademark of Superscape Limited
Thunder 100/C is trademark of Virtual Sys of Milano-Italy
Windows is trademark of Microsoft Corporation
WorldToolKit is trademark of SENSE8 Corporation
VR4 is trademark of Virtual Reality Incorporated
VREAM and VRCreator are trademarks of VREAM Incorporated
UNIX is a trademark of UNIX System Laboratories Incorporated

We would like to thank all of our loved ones who have given us the encouragement to start such a demanding endeavor. We dedicate this book to them.

❖ ❖ ❖

Acknowledgments

The authors wish to express their gratitude to Dr. Nazir Warsi for his personal as well as technical advice and encouragement; Dr. David Mizell of Boeing Computer Services and Mr. Vito DeMonte of the U.S. Army Research Laboratory for their continuous support. The authors also extend their gratitude to Dr. Larry Hodges, Mr. Eric Brittian, and Mr. Rob Kooper for their virtual reality expertise; and Dr. Barbara Rothbaum, Dr. Jim Williford and Dr. Dan Opdyke for conducting and evaluating therapy sessions for one of the pilot studies, Fear of Heights. Special thanks go to Mr. H. Trussell Pyle and Mrs. Anne German Wilson for their invaluable editing of this book and related publications.

We also extend our thanks to Dr. Kay Stanney for her direct contribution to the chapter on safety issues of virtual reality technology; Dr. Joseph Psotka and Dr. Sharon Davison for their major contributions to the chapters on virtual reality technology and the complementary research in the area of the cognitive aspects of virtual reality; Dr. Giuseppe Riva and Dr. Dorothy Strickland for their innovative research that contributes to the new paradigm of virtual reality therapy; Dr. Kalman Glantz, Dr. Nathaniel Durlach, Dr. Rosalind Barnett, and Mr. Walter Aviles for their contribution to the chapter concerning the future of virtual reality therapy; and Miss Aretha Edling for introducing the application of virtual reality to counseling methods. We thank Dr. Luciano L'Abate for his informal review of the first chapter. We also acknowledge all the other researchers who devoted their valuable time to pursue this line of research activities.

The research projects described in this book that were conducted at Clark Atlanta University were sponsored by several grants from Boeing Computer Services (Virtual Systems Department), U.S. Army Research Laboratory under contract DAAL03-92-6-0377, and supported by the Emory University and Georgia Institute of Technology Biomedical Technology Research Center (for the collaborative research of the fear of heights). The views contained in this document are those of the authors and should not be interpreted as representing the official policies of the U.S. government, either expressed or implied.

❖ ❖ ❖

Preface

Our initial publication of the first known research study in the use of virtual reality technology to combat psychological disorders brought many inquiries from scientists, clinicians, academicians, and patients suffering from psychological disorders. Although our research reports have been published by several scientific journals and been widely covered by the media, including the *New York Times, U.S. News & World Report, Atlanta Journal and Constitution, Psychiatric News (APA), Profile Magazine, PBS, ABC, and NBC,* it appears there is a great need to gather and present them in book form.

This book is a collection of current research activities that provide an innovative paradigm in psychotherapy which we term Virtual Reality Therapy (VRT). It is presented in a simple and understandable style for all the people who have inquired about it or may be interested in it. We hope this will encourage others to pursue further research into VRT, and that it will inspire other advancements and greater insights into this line of research. The participation of other scientists in our research efforts will contribute to our primary goal of improving the human condition.

The book is divided into twelve chapters. In Chapter One, we introduce and report on our discovery of VRT and preview the research efforts to establish the VRT paradigm. Chapter Two provides a brief introduction to the behavior therapy school of thought, and reports on traditional treatments of phobias (e.g., agoraphobia). Chapter Three introduces the technology of virtual reality; it focuses on immersion as a key factor in virtual reality therapy and begins to explore the different elements that contribute to immersion.

The purpose of the book is to make clear that an important new form of psychotherapy is taking shape, one of tremendous scientific potential. The book offers an extended overview of existing research on Virtual Reality Therapy, showing progress being made in the treatment of phobias, including fear of flying, agoraphobia and acrophobia; and in the treatment of eating disorders and autism. These research projects are reported in Chapters Four, Five, Six and Seven, respectively. Chapter Eight describes important and complementary research activities that have had a major impact on the advancement of VRT, explaining why and how this innovative technology works. Safety issues of virtual reality are discussed in Chapter Nine. Chapter Ten attempts to provide readers with the major assertions concerning virtual presence in VRT. Introduced in Chapters Eleven and Twelve are ongoing and future research projects to combat other psychological disorders. Among these are fear of public speaking, Obsessive-Compulsive Disorder, Attention Deficit Disorder, and Post-Traumatic Stress Disorder. Also discussed are experiences with augmented reality therapy and group therapy using computer networks (e.g., Internet).

This ground-breaking effort only scratches the surface of a vast uncharted area. It will take many more innovations, and many more trials and errors to arrive at the point of fully utilizing virtual reality in the majority of psychological disorders. Perhaps it will take even longer to develop VRT systems that can be used by patients as self-healing machines.

We hope this book will shed light on the VRT research and set direction for this new paradigm. We thank God for investing in us the ability to make this discovery, exploit its potential and disseminate our findings for the benefit of the scientific community and, ultimately, of humankind.

A Note on Terminology

The following terms are used interchangeably: therapist, psychologist, counselor and psychotherapist; client, patient, and subject; therapy and psychotherapy; virtual reality and virtual environment; and VED (Virtual Environment Desensitization), and VRT (Virtual Reality Therapy). For ease of reading, all the unknown third person references are "she".

❖ ❖ ❖

Contents

CHAPTER 1

Background

A MOMENT OF DISCOVERY

In November 1992, while testing a virtual reality experiment using one of our co-researchers in a virtual reality scene, we discovered that she experienced emotional and physical symptoms that resembled the experiences of a person reacting to a phobia. The virtual reality experiment, testing navigation software designed by an advanced graduate student, was a research project called "flying carpet." In this experimental scene, the participant "flies" in the direction she has chosen by physically stepping in that direction. It was observed that she became very uncomfortable and hesitant about flying in this virtual scene. When she was prompted, for example, to step forward to activate the forward flying motion, she started to shake and developed severe dizziness, stomach discomfort and sweaty palms. Some people react to prolonged exposure to virtual reality by experiencing what is termed simulation sickness. What she was experiencing were not the symptoms of simulation sickness but symptoms which arise from fear of flying, a phobia. For many years, other virtual reality researchers and laboratory technicians have observed symptoms of discomfort that they called simulation sickness. In this case, however, the symptoms were different. After our observations and discussions with other researchers, it was concluded that her symptoms were definitely those of a phobia.

THE FIRST PILOT STUDY

For the next several weeks we asked her to participate in the same virtual reality scene several times a week. We observed that she experienced similar emotions and physical symptoms each time. At this point, we were very excited about our discovery and invited students to participate in the experiment. Several volunteer students reported symptoms quite similar to those of the co-researcher. When asked if they had a fear of flying, these students confirmed that they did. To test our newly formed hypothesis that virtual reality can generate stimuli similar to a real world situation for phobic persons, an eight-session treatment plan was developed. It was similar to traditional systematic desensitization therapy and in vivo techniques commonly used by behavioral therapists. In the first session, our co-researcher was asked to wear the head-mounted computer graphics display terminal and to look around without trying to navigate within the virtual reality scene. She was directed to report her anxiety level by using a modified measure, Subjective Units of Disturbance (SUD) Scale (Wolpe, 1961). The modified SUD scale was an eleven point measure that ranged from 0 (total calm) to 10 (total panic). She was kept in this situation until her anxiety level decreased to zero. For the second session, she was asked to fly forward by physically stepping forward. Navigation in the virtual world was under her control. She could stop flying forward by simply stepping backward. At the beginning of each session, her anxiety increased and gradually decreased while she remained in that virtual reality scene. After eight sessions, she reported that she felt more comfortable flying in different directions (forward, backward, left and right, and combinations of these directions).

The second hypothesis, that her exposure and desensitization in virtual reality would transfer to the real world situation, was put to an empirical test. Accompanied by a therapist, she was flown by helicopter over the Gulf of Mexico for ten minutes. Though she experienced some discomfort, she reported less anxiety than she had experienced during a previous actual flying experience. It appeared that her virtual reality desensitization modified her fear memory structure and was transferred to the real world situation.

For the second phase of the experiment, she was asked to ride a parasail, a parachute that is raised in the air by a moving boat. It was expected that this experiment would produce much more anxiety than flying in an aircraft. As in the helicopter ride, she became anxious initially and then reported being much more comfortable during the ride. She said, "Now, I can really enjoy flying rather than constantly thinking about my fear." Since the parasail experiment, she has made several personal and professional trips by air. She reports that she is much more comfortable and has exhibited fewer anxiety-related symptoms (North and North, 1994).

THE DISCOVERY CONTINUED

Volunteer students were invited to participate in order to validate the hypotheses through on-going experimentation. It was observed that persons with a phobia exhibit avoidance and anxiety symptoms consistent with what they have experienced in real world situations. Surprisingly, several students experienced a variety of symptoms in other phobic areas, such as fear of closed places, fear of heights, and fear of animals.

FIRST KNOWN CONTROLLED STUDIES

In 1993, our discovery was shared with the Graphics Visualization and Usability (GVU) Center of Georgia Institute of Technology and the Psychiatric Division of the U.S. Army. While protecting the discovery as the intellectual property of Clark Atlanta University (CAU), the CAU team was successful in convincing the GVU and the U.S. Army's researchers that the CAU findings were valid and could easily be replicated in other laboratories. At that time, a consortium was formed to investigate the phenomena as applied to a specific phobia, fear of heights. Clinicians from Emory University and Georgia State University were invited to join the consortium. During weekly meetings, a controlled experiment was set up to empirically validate the CAU discovery. During this period, it was recommended by the CAU Human-Computer

Interaction Group that a controlled study be conducted with a larger population that would include a variety of phobic situations.

As a result of these deliberations, the Virtual Reality Technology Laboratory under the CAU Human-Computer Interaction Group was formed. Research in the use of virtual reality technology as a treatment for psychological disorders began in this laboratory. With the extended assistance of the U.S. Army Research Laboratory and continued support of Boeing Computer Services, the world's first known active Center for the Use of Virtual Reality Technology to Combat Psychological Disorders was formed.

CHANGE OF TERMS

The term Virtual Environment Desensitization (VED) was used initially in our research studies for the following reasons. (1) Traditional systematic desensitization technique and in vivo technique were being used for treatment of various phobias. (2) Recent contemporary literature in the virtual reality community used the term virtual environment. However, as this book will demonstrate, VED is neither a simple desensitization technique, nor an exposure therapy. It is a complex new paradigm that can be utilized in the treatment of other psychological disorders as well. With the new insights and the results reported by other researchers who have replicated or extended our original work to other areas of psychological disorders, the term Virtual Reality Therapy (VRT) is more explicit and accurate in describing this new paradigm. Because of our initial publications, some of which are reprinted here, the term VED appears in several sections of this book. For readers' convenience, both terms can be interpreted interchangeably.

THE VRT EXPERIMENTS

"Will virtual reality therapy successfully treat clients who suffer from phobias or other psychological disorders?" That was the major question for us to investigate. To provide some answers, several innovative research projects were designed and conducted. These research projects have become a primer for other researchers to follow.

In the initial study, VRT was shown to be remarkably effective in reducing the fear of flying and in improving the attitudes of several subjects toward flying. In the second study, VRT was shown to be effective in the treatment of persons with agoraphobia. These studies showed conclusively that persons with various phobias (fear of heights, open places, dark places, flying, etc.) could be treated successfully with VRT.

Currently, an extensive controlled experiment is being conducted by using a larger population to investigate the effectiveness of VRT in the treatment of a variety of psychological disorders. One of these experiments is developing virtual scenes to combat the fear of public speaking (social phobia).

In the following section is a preview of a few of our pilot studies.

Fear of Flying Experiments

Early case studies that revealed the success of VRT in treating phobias continue to serve as research models. The first one to assess the effectiveness of VRT in treatment of the fear of flying is a classic case. The pilot study, conducted in late November 1992, resulted from a fortuitous coincidence (North and North, 1994).

The subject, a 32-old married woman, was one of the CAU Human-Computer Interaction Group researchers looking into navigational techniques for virtual environments. The virtual scene on which she was working consisted of an aerial view of a simulated city running on a Silicon Graphics computer (Indigo). The navigational techniques she was helping to develop made her extremely nervous and fearful. Her severe reactions had all the marks of a phobia. That's when her colleagues began to suspect that her reactions were not just the common symptoms of simulation sickness.

The CAU researcher participated in eight closely observed therapy sessions, each of which lasted about 30 minutes. She reported a high level of anxiety at the beginning of each session and gradually reported lower levels of anxiety after remaining in the situation for a few minutes. She eventually reported an anxiety level of zero. To investigate the effect of VRT, accompanied by a therapist, she was flown by helicopter for approximately 10 minutes at a low altitude over a beach on the Gulf of Mexico. Similar to the VRT experience, she reported some anxiety at the beginning; however, the anxiety rapidly declined to a reasonably comfortable level. Currently, the researcher is much more comfortable flying for long distances and experiences much less anxiety.

The second early case study demonstrated the effectiveness of VRT in the treatment of a subject who also suffered from fear of flying (North, North and Coble, 1996a, 1997). In September 1995, this 42-year-old married man, who conducts research at CAU, sought treatment for himself. The subject's anxiety and avoidance behavior were interfering with his normal activities. He was unable to travel to professional conferences, visit relatives or take a vacation by air. Accompanied by a virtual therapist, the subject was placed in the cockpit of a virtual helicopter and flown over a simulated city for five sessions. The modified 11 point (0 means complete calm and 10 means complete panic) SUD rating measured the degree to which the subject was affected by VRT. In VRT, the subject's anxiety usually increased as he was exposed to more challenging situations and decreased as the time in that situation lengthened. The subject experienced a number of physical and anxiety-related symptoms during the VRT treatment sessions. These symptoms included sweaty palms, loss of balance and weakness in the knees. The VRT sessions resulted in both a significant reduction of anxiety symptoms and the ability to face the phobic situations that plagued him in the real world. The subject is now able to fly comfortably.

Agoraphobia Experiment

An unhealthy fear of being caught in places or situations from which escape may be difficult or embarrassing afflicts many people. This phobia, called agoraphobia, was ideally suited for a full scale VRT experiment.

This study at CAU was the first known controlled comprehensive assessment of the effectiveness of virtual reality technology in the treatment of psychological disorders (North, North and Coble, 1995a, 1995b, 1996c). The experiment began February 1, 1993. Sixty subjects were selected for the study. Thirty were placed in the experimental group and thirty were placed in the control group. Only subjects in the experimental group were exposed to VRT. The control group received no therapy. By the end of the study, the effectiveness of VRT in the treatment of agoraphobia was apparent. Attitudes toward agoraphobic situations decreased significantly for the VRT group but not for the control group. The average SUD rating in each session decreased steadily across sessions, indicating habituation.

Acrophobia Experiment

The first acrophobia study was conducted in collaboration with others (Williford, Hodges, North and North, 1993; Hodges, Kooper, Meyer, Rothbaum, Opdyke, DeGraaff, Williford and North, 1995; Rothbaum, Hodges, Opdyke, Kooper, Williford and North, 1995a, 1995b). The goal of this study was to investigate the efficacy of virtual reality graded exposure in the treatment of acrophobia. Twenty college students with fear of heights were randomly assigned to virtual reality graded exposure treatment or to a waiting list comparison group. Sessions were conducted with each individual alone over a period of eight weeks. The outcome was assessed by using measures of anxiety, avoidance, attitudes, and distress associated with exposure to heights before and after treatment. In all measures, significant differences were found among the subjects who completed the virtual reality treatment and subjects on the waiting list.

The second unique and in-depth case study demonstrates the effectiveness of VRT in the treatment of acrophobia (North and North, 1996b). After obtaining informed consent, the subject of this experiment was asked to rank a list of the acrophobic situations according to the degree of anxiety arousal. During the subject's first VRT session, he was familiarized with the virtual reality technology through several demonstrations. For the subject's subsequent eight sessions, which were between 15 and 28 minutes each, individual virtual reality treatment was conducted in a standard format. The first session began with the least threatening situation, conducted at ground level. The subject was placed near a virtual bridge that crossed a river in the middle of a simulated town. The SUD was administered every two to five minutes. The progress was totally under the subject's control, except when the subject's SUD score was zero. In this event, the experimenter urged the subject to move to the next level of the scene.

At one month post-treatment, the subject was asked to complete an eleven-point rating scale (including degrees for worsening symptoms) rating the degree to which his acrophobia symptoms have changed since the pre-treatment test (SUD). The subject experienced a number of physical anxiety symptoms during the VRT sessions. These symptoms included sweaty palms, loss of balance and weakness in the knees. The results indicated that the subject experienced significant habituation of anxiety symptoms and exercised less avoidance of phobic situations. Thus, we concluded that the VRT was successful in reducing fear of heights.

RELATED REPORTS OF VRT

November 1992 marked the beginning of the innovative VRT research studies. To date, those CAU studies remain the only known studies to document the effectiveness of VRT scientifically. Since then, there has been a growing interest in VRT. In Japan, virtual reality was used to simulate sand play projective techniques for autistic children (Kijima, Shirakawa, Hirsoe, and Nihei, 1993); however, no data were reported. It appeared to be a useful alternative to sand play but it did not constitute a treatment. In 1994, *CyberEdge Journal* reported on a study conducted by a Kaiser-Perminente researcher. Again, no data or ana-lytical results were presented.

In 1996, two reports of using virtual reality to assist persons with psychological disorders were presented at the *Medicine Meets Virtual Reality IV* Conference at San Diego (MMVR-IV, 1996). The first report dealt with a preliminary study of virtual reality and body experience, a new approach to the treatment of eating disorders. It was presented by Dr. Giuseppe Riva from Applied Technology for Psychology Labo-ratory in Intra, Italy. The second research paper, on the use of virtual reality to help children with autism, was presented by Dr. Dorothy Strickland of the North Carolina State University. This report included two case studies on providing a customized virtual learning environ-ment for individuals suffering from autism.

COMPLEXITY OF VRT

Reports of our discovery and use of our methods of VRT are spreading rapidly. VRT is growing in application and thus in complexity. Recently, a number of other researchers have recognized the potential and importance of this innovative therapy and have begun to .conduct similar research activities. Without exception, all of these researchers have reported positive and significant results. The fact that their efforts were conducted outside the CAU group further validates the research results of the CAU team. These successes attest to the fact that the new paradigm of VRT is so solid and powerful that the lack of procedural knowledge of the therapy does not significantly effect the outcome of the therapy. Some possible reasons for the effectiveness of this approach will be introduced in this section.

VRT is different from simple desensitization and exposure therapy as described by the behavioral schools of thought. VRT appears to be oriented more toward neurophysiological information processing theory (Bower, 1981; Lang, 1977, 1979) and the accelerated integrative information processing paradigm presented by Shapiro (1995). Thus far, the CAU team and others who have replicated their research have proven that VRT works very well with subjects who suffer from various kinds of phobias. Intuitive observation has also led to the belief that more than desensitization was at work. Clients were immersed in the virtual world; they typically would not communicate with therapists who reside in the physical world. They appeared to be reliving their previous disturbing or anxiety-provoking experiences even though the virtual world did not accurately match their existential world. They would usually look repeatedly at the same simple object or objects within the virtual world. Advanced graphics, while providing stronger immersion, seem to be distracting and overloading the human perceptual processing system and are not allowing the other cognitive processes, which are essential to problem solving and information reprocessing, to work efficiently (Psotka, Davison and Lewis,1993; Psotka and Davison, 1993; North, North and Coble, 1995a, 1995b, 1996a, 1996b, 1996c, 1997; Strickland, Marcus, Hogan, Mesibov, and McAllister, 1995). Based on our observation, the processes seem to be very similar to the treatment that

Shapiro (1995) calls EMDR (Eye Movement Desensitization Reprocessing).

Disturbing memory is stored by a picture, cognition, affect, and physical sensations. VRT reveals that these factors are stored by association and linked together. VRT appears to activate the visual memory, in case only visual stimuli are presented, and in turn activates other related memories and experiences such as cognition, affect, and physical sensation. Under VRT, many of the subjects report physical and emotional symptoms associated with these stored memories. They report having sweaty palms and shaking knees, feeling scared, and feeling uncomfortable. More details of emotional and physical symptoms experienced by clients will be covered later in this book.

In general, VRT appears to provide a link between the reality of the client and the objective world.However, at this time there is no concrete or empirically based evidence to explain why and how VRT works. Thus the great need for researchers to investigate the psychological mechanics of VRT. While other researchers are either replicating the CAU work or searching for new applications of VRT, the CAU team remains committed to exploring the nature of virtual reality therapy in the years to come.

CHAPTER 2

Behavioral Therapy

The primary goal of this chapter is to provide a brief introduction to the basic issues and techniques of the behavioral approach to psychotherapy and its use in the treatment of agoraphobia. Comprehensive coverage of behavioral therapy is not in the scope of this book. For more information, readers are encouraged to refer to specific resources, several of which are listed in the reference section of this book.

AN OVERVIEW OF BEHAVIORAL THERAPY

The behavioral approach to psychotherapy, a major school of thought in psychotherapy, is distinctly different from other psychological approaches. The behavioral approach does not use the long-held principle that the patient improves by talking, nor does it emphasize the importance of the therapy relationship. Behavioral therapy is a combination of related approaches which hold that "emotional, learning and adjustment difficulties can be treated through a variety of prescriptive, mechanical, usually non-dynamic techniques and procedures" (Belkin, 1988). The environmental factors that affect the individual's behavior are the focus of the behavioral approach to psychotherapy.

11

The behavioral approach is based on the learning theory, which assumes that the behavior of all humans is learned. Thus, behavior can be modified by learning an alternative way to deal with an anxiety-producing situation.

Since Wolpe's technique was extensively used in our pilot studies, we include his point of view here. Wolpe's definition of behavior therapy is "the use of experimentally established principles and paradigms of learning to overcome nonadaptive behavior" (Wolpe, 1982). Simply, Wolpe defines his therapy technique as motivating the client to perform responses antagonistic to anxiety. Details of his techniques are included in the following sections.

A BRIEF HISTORY OF BEHAVIORAL THERAPY

The empirical philosopher John Locke is generally acknowledged as the one who established the philosophical and psychological premises of the behavioral approach. Working independently, the behavioral approach was developed later in the United States of America by John B. Watson and Edward L. Thorndike.

In 1920, Watson and his colleague Roslind Rayner conditioned "Little Albert" to fear white rats by causing the child to associate a loud frightening noise with white rats. After a few such pairings, Albert developed a fear of rats even when the noise was not present. Gradually Albert developed a phobia for all furry objects (generalization). The most important point of this experiment is that if an organism can be conditioned to fear, then it can also be de-conditioned, removing the fear.

B. F. Skinner, another prominent scholar, is considered the most influential person in behavioral psychology. He contended that the effects of reinforcement and punishment are not symmetrical; reinforcement changes the probability of the recurrence of a response, but punishment does not (Skinner, 1971). Skinner's ideas and theories are widely used and are generally recognized as the most effective way of working with retarded or autistic children.

Joseph Wolpe, born in 1915, studied experimental neurosis in animals. He experimented with cats by using electric shock to induce neurotic reactions. After the electric shock was removed, the cats were induced to eat small and then increasingly larger units of an anxiety-evoking stimulus. As a result of the experiment, a conditional inhibition to the anxiety responses was established (Wolpe, 1958).

TECHNIQUES OF THERAPY

Behavior therapy utilizes a variety of individual techniques and combinations of techniques. The following are some of the techniques commonly used by therapists.

Cognitive Procedures

Cognitive activities are part of human interaction. All psychotherapy theories include some cognitive elements. "The behavior (output) in a given situation is determined by the input provided by the situation and by an evaluation of the situation. This is based, in part, on the memories of what had resulted in a similar situation" (Hergenhahn, 1988). Fear can be the outcome of misinformation about a situation, eliciting in the patient a reaction to an unreal danger. The patient's thinking can be changed by providing her with correct information. The patient must be informed that the therapist will help her to break the self-defeating, or fear-arousing habit.

Thought stopping

Thought stopping is a procedure that halts unrealistic, anxiety-producing or obsessive thoughts. The patient is asked to close her eyes and start the thought sequence. The therapist shouts "stop". The patient notices that the thought is gone. This procedure is repeated several times. Then the patient is ask to practice stopping thoughts by saying "stop" to herself.

Assertiveness Training

Wolpe (1982) defines assertive behavior as the proper expression of any emotion other than anxiety toward another person. Inner turmoil arises from suppressing one's feelings. The patient must accept that she needs to be assertive and that this assertiveness is not in conflict with her ethical or religious training. In general, the patient must learn to assert herself by placing herself first, although not necessarily to the detriment of others who should also be considered.

Systematic Desensitization

Systematic desensitization involves having the patient imagine anxiety-evoking scenes rather than actually experiencing them. During the experiment, the patient is given step-by-step instructions for breaking down habits of neurotic anxiety-inducing responses (Patterson, 1986; Wolpe, 1982). The therapy starts by having the patient relax. Next she is exposed to a weak stimulus that invokes anxiety. Stronger stimuli are introduced systematically as the previous ones are reduced. This procedure is continued until the maximum anxiety-arousing stimuli ceases to have an effect on the patient and the zero anxiety point is reached.

The patient is trained in relaxation techniques that take about six or seven sessions. The relaxation techniques begin with the arm muscles, followed by the head and face, neck and shoulders, back, abdomen, thorax, and lower limbs. At the conclusion of the sessions, an anxiety hierarchy is constructed. This is a list of anxiety-arousing stimuli, listed according to the degree of anxiety they produce. The hierarchy listing is normally constructed from the patient's responses to the Willoughby Personality Schedule (WPS), the Fear Survey Schedule, and the therapist's observation. It is not essential that the patient experiences anxiety. An imaginary situation can be substituted instead. In order to build a scale of 0 to 100, the patient is asked a series of anxiety-evoking questions.

Drugs like diazepam or codeine may be given to patients who cannot relax completely. Carbon dioxide-oxygen mixtures, hypnotism or having the patient imagine relaxing scenes may also be helpful. When the patient is relaxed, she is asked to visualize the least anxiety-evoking situation in the WPS hierarchy. The patient is asked to raise a finger if she sees the scene clearly. This situation is stopped after 5 to 7 seconds when the therapist says, "Stop the scene." Using the scale of 0 to 100, the therapist asks the patient to rate the degree of anxiety produced by the imagined scene. This procedure is repeated until the anxiety-arousal from each scene is reduced to zero.

After patients have been desensitized to the hierarchy scenes through the use of imagination procedures, they are exposed to the actual stimulus (in vivo technique). In this procedure, the therapist is an active participant in the anxiety-arousing situation.

Wolpe's procedure requires the patient to introspect about the content and intensity of her negative emotional states and to think, reason, remember, judge, discriminate and imagine. Neither hierarchy construction nor muscle relaxation are necessary elements of Wolpe's procedure. Imagination of the fear-relevant scene is the only necessary element for Wolpe's procedure.

Aids to Systematic Desensitization

Several methods can reduce therapy time. The most utilized techniques are:

Mechanical Aids to Systematic Desensitization

To help the patient relax, relaxation instructions are given on a special tape recorder, after which there is a pause. Then the patient is asked to visualize the first scene. There is a ten second silence. After the period of silence, the patient is instructed to stop visualizing. If any anxiety exists, the repeat button is pressed, which rewinds the tape to the beginning. If there is no anxiety, the tape continues to the next relaxation directions, the second scene is visualized and so on. A simple version of the tape is also made available.

Group Desensitization

Group therapy has been quite successful in desensitization. Patients with the same neuroses may be effectively treated in a group setting. This also reduces the cost of treatment.

Conditioning Induced by Shock Stimuli

Another method of therapy is to condition the patient to a neutral stimulus word, such as "relax." The patient is then given an unpleasant shock which is stopped when she says the word "relax."

Desensitization In Vivo

Desensitization in vivo means asking the client to expose herself to the actual stimulus. In vivo is a suitable alternative for clients who have trouble imagining scenes or responding emotionally to the imagined scenes. With the assistance of the therapist, graded exposure to real stimuli is an effective technique to desensitize the client.

Operant Conditioning

Wolpe considers positive reinforcement, negative reinforcement, and extinction as three primary operant conditioning techniques. Positive reinforcement refers to establishing a habit by providing a reward or reinforcement for each or many of its performances. Negative reinforcement refers to the removal of an unpleasant stimulus, often introduced by a therapist, which strengthens the desired response. Extinction is the repetition of a response, to the point of exhaustion, that comes without reinforcement.

Modeling

Bandura (1977) has studied the effectiveness of modeling in treating psychological disorders. Bandura demonstrated that, both direct modeling (seeing a live model) and symbolic modeling (seeing a model in a film) are both effective in reducing fears. He further demonstrates that direct modeling, with participation, is more effective.

Use of Chemical Agents

Drugs such as benzodiazepines, alprozalam (Xanax) and clonazepam (Klonopine), are prescribed to reduce anxiety. Other, such as imipramine (Iofranil), desipramine (Norpramin), nortriptylline (Pamelor),beta-blockers (Inderal and Tenormin), and serotonin (Prozac and Zoloft), are known for suppressing anxiety that creates physical arousal immediately before encountering an anxiety-evoking situation.

Aversion Therapy

Aversion therapy is the practice of inhibiting an undesired response by administering an aversive stimulus coincident with an undesired response. This treatment is specially useful in the treatment of obsessions, compulsions, and fetishes (Patterson, 1986). Electric stimulation and drugs have also been used in aversion treatment (for example, the aversion treatment of alcoholism).

Behavioral Self-control Programs

From a practical standpoint, behavioral changes and modifications must persist after the treatment. For this reason, behavior professionals have focused a great deal of effort on behavioral self-control programs. These behavioral self-control programs emphasize the importance of having the patient monitor and control her own behavior, during and after the program (Belkin, 1988).

Other Techniques

There are several other techniques that deal specifically with evoking strong anxiety. The most pronounced ones are abreaction, flooding, and paradoxical intention, which are not within the scope of this text. For additional information, other psychological references and the technological resources included in the reference section of this book should be consulted.

NATURE OF AGORAPHOBIA

Recent studies report that anxiety disorders are frequently found in the general population. Most disorders in this group occur among first-degree biological relatives. For example, it has been reported that agoraphobia is the most common anxiety disorder. Agoraphobia is also one of the most serious and prevalent anxiety disorders in the field of mental health. It is responsible for approximately 60% of all phobic disorder sufferers who seek treatment. Extensive epidemiological studies reveal that between 2.7% and 5.8% of the population (5-11 million) suffer from agoraphobia (Meyers, Weissman, Tischler, Holzer, Leaf, Orvaschel, Anthony, Boyd, Burke, Kraemer, and Stoltzman, 1984; Weissman, 1985). The percentage are much higher for specific phobias. For example, according to an internal report by the Boeing Company, over 25 million people in the United States are afraid to fly, and 20 percent of those who have to fly on a regular basis rely on sedatives or alcohol during flights to help them deal with the fear.

Unfortunately, the exposure-based treatment has only an approximately 50% success rate. This does not include non-respondents and subjects who are unable to complete treatment. This relatively useful technique and its variants cannot be considered a panacea for agoraphobia or other phobias (Michelson, Mavissakalian and Marchione, 1985; Russell, 1992). It is incumbent upon researchers to continue to develop and empirically test more effective treatments for phobias and other psychological disorders.

Since our first known extensive controlled investigation of VRT has dealt with patients who suffer from agoraphobia, a working definition will be provided. Agoraphobia is an abnormally intense fear of being in places or situations from which escape might be difficult or embarrassing. People having this disorder suffer from marked distress about having the fear or from significant behavior difficulties. This behavior dysfunction often causes interference with normal routine and interpersonal relationships. Agoraphobia can result in significant distress in any setting.

People who suffer from agoraphobia restrict their activities away from home. These include activities that involve crowds, being on bridges, being in elevators, and using public or private transportation. Victims of agoraphobia suffer a limited number of symptoms. They can develop only a single symptom or a number of physical and psychological symptoms. These symptoms may include dizziness, falling, loss of bladder or bowel control, vomiting, cardiac distress, depersonalization or derealization. In most cases the symptoms have occurred in the past, and the person anticipates their recurrence. An additional symptom of fear is the anticipation of humiliation or embarrassment in specific situations. Therefore, the phobic person tries to avoid situations that may provoke the anxiety.

The level to which anxiety may increase or decrease can be predicated by the location or nature of the phobic stimulus (e.g., height of a building).

There have been a few investigations conducted to determine how agoraphobia should be categorized among panic disorders and how it should be classified when the *Diagnostic and Statistical Manual of Mental Disorders* is revised. (See article by Goisman, Warshaw, Steketee, Fierman, Rogers, Goldenberg, Weinshenker, Vasile, and Keller, 1995 for a detailed discussion of the agoraphobia disorder). The current issue of the *Diagnostic and Statistical Manual of Mental Disorders*, Fourth Edition (American Psychiatric Association, 1994), describes the diagnostic criteria for agoraphobia (300.22 Agoraphobia without history of panic disorder) this way:

A. The presence of Agoraphobia is related to the fear of developing panic-like symptoms (e.g., dizziness or diarrhea).
B. Criteria have never been met for panic disorder.
C. The disturbance is not due to the direct physiological effects of a substance (e.g., a drug of abuse, a medication) or a general medical condition.

D. If an associated general medical condition is present, the fear described in Criterion A is clearly in excess of that usually associated with the condition.

TRADITIONAL TREATMENTS FOR AGORAPHOBIA

One of the major techniques used in the behavioral approach to counseling and psychotherapy is systematic desensitization. The technique of systematic desensitization is based upon the learning principle of reciprocal inhibition, which was developed by Wolpe (1958). Wolpe defines reciprocal inhibition as follows: Reciprocal inhibition means that if a relaxing response is paired with an anxiety-producing stimulus, a new bond develops between the two so that the anxiety-provoking stimulus no longer provokes anxiety (Belkin, 1988).

In other words, systematic desensitization eliminates fear because fear is incompatible with relaxation. Systematic desensitization consists of two components: (1) the relaxation component that teaches the client to adopt a mental set of relaxation; and (2) the imaginal component that teaches the client to visualize the anxiety-producing scene systematically.

Stronger stimuli are gradually invoked as the previous ones are reduced to zero anxiety and, until the maximum anxiety-arousing stimulus has no effect on the patient's responses. Finally, patients are encouraged to experience real world situations.

Garvey and Hegrenes (1966) described systematic desensitization by providing an excellent case study that shows how a school psychologist treated a child suffering from school phobia—a disorder that responds well to the systematic desensitization technique. A ten-year-old boy was not able to enter the car in which he travels to school. The planned systematic desensitization consisted of twelve graduated stages. The psychologist accompanied the boy in every stage. When the boy felt comfortable at a certain stage, the next step was applied, and so on. These were the stages:

- Getting into the car that was parked in front of the school.
- Getting out of the car and approaching the curb.

- Going to the sidewalk.
- Going to the bottom of the school steps.
- Going to the top of the steps.
- Going to the door.
- Entering the school.
- Approaching the classroom from a certain distance each day.
- Entering the classroom.
- Being present in the classroom with the teacher.
- Being present in the classroom with the teacher and one or two classmates.
- Being present in the classroom with the full class.

COMPARATIVE STUDIES OF TREATMENT FOR AGORAPHOBIA

The scope of this book does not permit concentrating on the traditional techniques for treatment of agoraphobia or other specific phobias, therefore this section briefly provides only a select number of comparative studies which explore treatments for phobias. These studies include Exposure Systematic Desensitization, In Vivo, Pharmacological, Cognitive, and a more innovative approach, Lens-based Desensitization. Also, it must be noted that only a few comparative studies have been conducted to evaluate the effectiveness of different techniques to combat phobias, specifically agoraphobia.

Michelson, Mavissakalian and Marchione (1985) reported on cognitive and behavioral treatments of agoraphobia, its clinical, behavioral, and psychological outcomes. In this study, thirty-nine severe and chronic agoraphobic patients with panic disorders were diagnosed according to the DSM III (American Psychiatric Association, 1980) and randomly assigned to three different treatment techniques: cognitive-behavioral treatments which included paradoxical intention, graded exposure, and progressive deep muscle relaxation training. Experienced therapists conducted a treatment of 12 two-hour weekly sessions. In addition to the primary treatment, subjects were given instructions that emphasized self-directed exposure and programmed practice. A battery of assessment questions was administered at pre-treatment (six weeks), post-treatment (twelve weeks) and at follow-up (three months). This included clinical ratings of severity, phobia, anxiety, depression, and panic, as well as direct measure of behavioral, psychophysiological and cognitive response systems. Behavioral assessment such as heart rate measures and motion sensors were used. There were no significant initial differences, due to treatments, on any of the assessment domains — clinical or behavioral. Additionally, no significant differences were found among the groups on any of the pretreatment demographic, clinical, or historical measures. Analysis of the data revealed statistically significant differences across treatments. Subjects in all conditions improved significantly in anxiety, phobia, depression, behavioral functioning, and panic attack measures. The Graded Exposure and Progressive Deep Muscle Relaxation techniques appeared to produce more rapid effects.

In another comparative research study, Michelson, Mavissakalian and Marchione (1985) investigated the relative and combined effectiveness of behavior therapy, prolonged in vivo exposure, and pharmacological treatment using imipramine, on sixty-two severe and chronic agoraphobic subjects. Assessments were conducted at pretreatment, four weeks, eight weeks, twelve weeks, and at the one month post-treatment periods. The preliminary results of their data analysis yielded significant findings with regard to both process and clinical outcome.

Pendleton and Higgins (1983) conducted a comparative study of negative and systematic desensitization in the treatment of acrophobia. Twenty-one acrophobia subjects from the community were randomly assigned to one of three treatment conditions—negative practice, desensitization, and relaxation only, or to a controlled waiting list. Negative practice helps clients learn to control their anxiety symptoms by learning to produce them voluntarily. The Acrophobia Questionnaire (Cohen, 1977) and Acrophobia Behavioral Tests were administered for pre-testing and post-testing sessions. Treatment procedures consist of six weekly 45-minute sessions. Results from several self-reported measures and a behavioral measure indicated that negative practice and desensitization were equally effective in the treatment. The relaxation only treatment was much less effective, but produced some improvement.

The efficacy of imaginal and in vivo desensitization in the treatment of agoraphobia has been investigated by James, Hampton, May, and Larsen (1983). They report that many claims have been made that in vivo procedures are normally superior to imaginal approaches in the treatment of anxiety disorders. Such claims seem unwarranted. Six agoraphobic women (mean age of 44.7 years) participated in a study that utilized a multi-baseline single-subject methodology. These anxieties were spontaneous panic attacks, high levels of general anxiety and avoidance of going out-of-doors, public transportation, and being in crowds. The phobia's severity was assessed by using avoidance behavior, subjective distress, and the subjects' self-monitored pulse rate. An analysis of the data showed significant reductions in phobic behavior during imaginal and in vivo desensitization without supporting the position that, of the two methods, one is superior to the other. The results of the study indicate that the imaginal and in vivo procedures were equally effective in reducing observed avoidance behavior and subjective distress. In general, the results of this study did not follow the previous suggestion that in vivo exposure is necessarily superior to imaginal desensitization in the treatment of agoraphobic clients.

Rossi and Seiler (1990) reported a comparative study that investigated the comparative effectiveness of systematic desensitization and an interrogative approach in treating public speaking anxiety. The foundation for the integrative approach is that subjects are instructed to engage in a mental rehearsal process that would transform the negative experience into a positive one (Ayres and Hopf, 1985). This study adopted a multi modal approach, including passive progressive muscle relaxation, deep breathing, and visualization, to treat the anxiety. Twelve subjects, eight males and four females, were selected and divided between the two treatment groups. Measures such as Speech Trait Anxiety, Speech State Anxiety and Physiology were used in this study. The physiological measures included skin temperature, galvanic skin response, electromyograph, systolic blood pressure, diastolic blood pressure, and heart rate. During the pre-test and post-test phases each subject was seated in a classroom in front of the instructor's desk for four weeks. The results are still inconclusive but they showed strong evidence to suggest that both treatments can reduce trait and state anxiety. The integrative approach appears to be the more effective in decreasing the symptoms associated with public speaking anxiety disorder.

The most innovative research, probably the only research of its kind, in the treatment of acrophobia was conducted in 1982. John Schneider reported a case study of a 40-year-old married man who sought treatment for anxiety related to heights. He was treated by an innovative lens-assisted in vivo desensitization technique. Although in vivo systematic desensitization appears to be highly effective, it requires exposure to stimuli that are difficult to control during the therapy. Creatively, Schneider utilized optical lenses to alter perceived depth and distance for the treatment of his subject. In reality, he reversed the view through ordinary binoculars which offers a simple means for achieving this effect. The subject suffered from a primary fear of heights that caused him to have a severe aversion to flying as well. His anxiety and avoidance behaviors were significantly interfering with his professional and social activities. Unable to fly to professional and personal trips was the most disturbing effect of the phobia for the client. Following relaxation training, a windowed interior stairwell of an eight story building was used for desensitization. The subject was treated for three one-hour weekly sessions. At each level, the subject was asked to look out of the window to the ground below by using the binoculars in the reverse viewing fashion. This magnified the apparent distance much more than it really was (seven times more). The viewing trials were repeated at each level until the anxiety rating, decreased to 3 or less (on a scale of 0-10) for three consecutive viewings. The procedure was repeated at a higher elevation. The treatment was terminated when the subject successfully climbed the actual eight stories and mastered the apparent height of about 56 stories. Eight months after the treatment and in a follow-up interview, data indicated the maintenance of treatment efforts.

CHAPTER 3

Virtual Reality Technology

This chapter covers only the components of virtual reality that are essential to the background and understanding of VRT. Readers interested in comprehensive coverage of virtual reality technology are encouraged to consult other resources (see reference section). Most of the information in this chapter has been provided by Dr. Joseph Psotka, director of the U.S. Army Research Institute, and it reflects his point of view on virtual reality technology. In this chapter you will find a short history of virtual reality, several definitions and applications, and some technical aspects of its components and architecture. It also deals with the most important psychological experiences of immersion. There is a short section on the Affordability of this technology.

A BRIEF HISTORY OF VIRTUAL REALITY

Most of the pioneering research in virtual reality can be traced back to 1960 and the work of Ivan Sutherland. In 1965, Sutherland designed the first head-mounted computer-graphics display device that also tracked the position of the wearer's head. This marked the beginning of virtual reality research and applications. Sutherland postulated that:

> *"The ultimate display would, of course, be a room within which the computer could control the existence of matter. A chair displayed in such a room would be good enough to sit in. Handcuffs displayed in such a room would be confining, and a bullet displayed in such a room would be fatal."*

In 1967, Frederick Brooks of the University of North Carolina began an extensive study to explore force feedback utilizing computers. Force feedback directs physical pressure or force through a computer interface to the user so that the user can feel computer-simulated forces. This line of research contributed significantly to the current state of virtual reality user interfaces.

The next technological advances occurred in 1972 when Nolan Bushnell introduced Pong, the first interactive electronic game. It allowed the player to interact with a bouncing ping-pong ball displayed on a TV screen.

In the mid-eighties, the Ames Research Center at NASA started the development of a relatively low-cost virtual reality head-mounted display from a Liquid Crystal Display TV. This new low-cost technology made virtual reality technology affordable and reachable for other researchers in the field. After a very slow technological advancement period (1986-1988) in the field of virtual reality, many researchers began to revisit this technology. Today, virtual reality research is conducted by government, industry, academia and individual researchers. Many researchers see virtual reality as a way to meet human needs by creating intelligent, people-centered products with applications in business, education, entertainment, medicine and health care.

VIRTUAL REALITY APPLICATIONS

In spite of current virtual reality systems limitations, the technology has caught the imagination of many people. It is a sophisticated integration of a number of technologies, and seems capable of becoming a significant tool in a number of applications. The types of applications that may be utilizing virtual reality in the future is an open question (Bryson, 1992).

Recently, practical applications of virtual reality have extended to many diverse areas. A glimpse of the current research in virtual reality reveals work on a database that will enable users to "see" the database as a three-dimensional (3-D) model. By wearing a glove and a headset, the user can manipulate the data and its links. For example, the network administrator, wearing goggles and a glove, can work in 3-D images of a computer-generated network grid. Other areas of research include product design and modeling in the areas of pharmaceuticals, bio-technology, and medical applications such as surgical simulation and psychotherapy.

VIRTUAL REALITY: WHAT IS IT?

With the technology in its infancy, there are many different and varied definitions of virtual reality. Thomas Furness (1993) puts it this way:

"Virtual Environment technology provides a medium through which computers can generate three dimensional worlds into which humans can enter. These worlds consist of three dimensional objects which can be seen, heard, and touched but which are virtual projects into the senses."

Sheridan(1992) offers a definition of virtual reality from the human-computer interaction point of view. According to Sheridan, virtual reality offers a new human-computer interaction paradigm in which users are no longer simply external observers of data or images on a computer screen. They are active participants within a computer-generated, three-dimensional virtual world. Virtual reality differs from traditional displays in that computer graphics and various display and input technologies are integrated to give the user a sense of presence or immersion in the virtual world.

Newquist (1992) defines virtual reality as a technology that enables users to enter computer-generated worlds and interface with them three-dimensionally through sight, sound, and touch. Bryson (1992) reports that virtual reality also provides special techniques that allow users to interact with virtual spaces. Current techniques include the use of special gloves that track hand and finger positions so that the user can grasp virtual objects, six-degrees-of-freedom mouse, navigation devices and locomotive devices such as treadmills, bicycles, or "flying" chairs that allow users to move about in the environment.

Although there are many working definitions for virtual reality, one of the simplest and most powerful is offered by Burdea and Coiffet (1994) in their recent book, "Virtual Reality Technology" which gives the three "I"s of virtual reality. The three "I"s make a triangle of Immersion, Interaction, and Imagination. Most virtual reality researchers and enthusiasts are familiar with the first two "I"s which are essentially what makes a virtual reality system. The introduction of the third "I" by Burdea and Coiffet, as you will see in the remainder of this book, makes their interpretation and philosophy of virtual reality unique and innovative. This definition of virtual reality will be complemented by our empirical data that supports the belief that imagination (or what the user brings to the environment), compared to immersion and interaction, is the most important feature of any virtual reality system.

KINDS OF VIRTUAL REALITY

There are two kinds of virtual reality; although in some ways, they are complementary and not really distinguishable. The two basic varieties are sensory immersive virtual reality and text-based networked virtual reality. This book will deal mainly with visually immersive virtual reality, the kind that makes your view of the world change when you move your head. Another variety of virtual reality is desktop virtual reality or "fish tank virtual reality" (Ware, Kevin, and Kellogg, 1993). It can be treated as another form of simulation technology. Though similar to immersive virtual reality, the main difference is that desktop or "fish tank" virtual reality partitions a smaller amount of the surrounding space.

IMMERSIVE VIRTUAL REALITY

Immersive virtual reality can be defined by its technology and effects. Its primary effect is to place a person into a simulated environment that looks and feels like the real world (see Figure 1). A person in this synthetic environment has a sense of self-location, can move her head and eyes to explore it, feels that the space surrounds her, and can interact with objects in the synthetic environment. In immersive virtual reality, simulated objects appear solid and have an egocentric location, much like real objects in the real world. The objects can be picked up, examined from all sides, navigated around, heard, smelled, touched, lifted, and explored in many sensory ways. The objects can also be autonomous (especially if they are other people) and can interact with the virtual voyager or respond to voice commands (Middleton and Boman, 1994). The fundamental limitation to all these effects is in the computational technology that supports them.

THE TECHNOLOGY OF VIRTUAL REALITY

The technology of virtual reality is rapidly changing and improving within the research community. The following sections discuss some of the more important components of this technology for current working environments.

Head-Mounted Display

The essential ingredient of virtual reality is a tracked head-mounted display (HMD) that lets you see the visual world as you move your head. Wearing a HMD, one can look around and see the rest of the simulated world. Current image generation computers are limited in their ability to create a realistic, changing world. Special image generators cost more than a hundred thousand dollars. The special lightweight, high-resolution displays can be equally as expensive. Current microcomputers can realistically generate about 100 thousand polygons per second, while it has been estimated that nearly a billion polygons per second may be needed for near realism. The lack of sufficient funding for the necessary technology not only leads to low resolution and cartoon-like shapes, but it also leads to long lags of hundreds of milliseconds between changes in the head position and updates of the display. Narrow fields of view (often about half the normal field of view of 180 degrees) lead to distortions of perceived space, inaccurate

self-localization (Psotka, Davison and Lewis, 1993), errors in the judgment of distances (Henry and Furness, 1993), and simulator sickness
(feelings of discomfort that can range from mild eyestrain and headaches to nausea and vomiting).

However, based on our research and the research of others, the
virtual worlds used in VRT do not have to match the real world
situations in order to invoke appropriate stimuli in the subjects. Thus,
the low-end virtual reality system, even with cartoon-like shapes, seems
to be enough to create an anxiety-evoking scene for the subjects.

Tracking

An unobtrusive tracking mechanism (magnetic, mechanical, infrared,
gyroscopic, sound or innovative alternatives) registers any head motion
and provides the signals to a computer to make the required changes in
viewpoint in the modelled display. When your head moves, the visual
scene changes. The result is a change of viewpoint just as if the eyes
and head had moved in the virtual world. In an expensive advanced
system, when your eyes move, the scene changes. Such eye tracking is
often used to provide a more detailed "fovea" or Area Of Interest (AOI)
display (Warner, Serfoss and Hubbard, 1993) of high resolution imagery that tracks the viewpoint. Any of these tracked displays usually
result in a compelling sense of "being there," of being immersed in the
simulation as if it were the real world. Unfortunately, long lags between
the user's action and the resulting computed change in the display often
destroys this illusion and can lead to simulator sickness.

Gestures and Force Feedback

The use of gloves to make gestures and interact with objects and force-
reflective feedback can create a compelling experience. The core of the
experience is primarily visual. Tactile reinforcement of the presence of
an object, its shape, weight, solidity, and texture, adds to the experience.

Force feedback about collisions with objects is a fundamental aid to
navigation in virtual reality. It prevents you from going through walls,
the floor, and other objects. Otherwise such sudden unnatural transitions

often lead to disorientation and confusion. Gestures based on the sensing of hand position and shape provide a natural means for interacting and communicating with the computer. For instance, one can select a distant object by pointing at it. Sometimes this selection is facilitated by having a ray extrude from a finger to the object. Others have suggested that one should be able to select objects by throwing something at them.

Stereo Sound

Localizing objects from a stereo sound adds to the sense of presence and immersion. Unfortunately, accurate localization depends on the shape of each individual's pinna or outer ear, so only ambiguous localization is currently possible. In either case, the experience is still quite compelling.

Voice Synthesis and Recognition

Voice input and output capabilities are progressing rapidly and may soon be added to general virtual reality environments, but remain largely unexploited. Middleton and Boman (1994) have conducted a practically and theoretically ground breaking study of the conditions in a virtual reality environment where voice recognition is useful. They observed that voice is best used for discrete changes in the environment, such as, "Put me near object X", but not as good for continuously varying dynamic dimensions such as the direction or speed of one's flight.

Sense of Smell

There are many different ways to use odors to create a striking sense of presence. The technology of delivering odors is well-developed (Varner, 1993) in trials at Southwest Research Institute. The odors are all Food and Drug Administration approved and delivered at low concentration. The system uses a microencapsulation technique that can be dry packaged in cartridges that are safe and easy to handle. Human chemical senses such as taste and smell create particularly salient memories. They are also useful for alerting us to danger, sexual arousal, and emotional experience.

THE PSYCHOLOGICAL EXPERIENCE OF IMMERSION

In spite of the many technological limitations of virtual reality, many virtual reality environments create a compelling sense of "being there," of presence or immersion. The psychological and human interface issues that affect immersion are being analyzed by several experimenters (Barfield and Weghorst, 1993; Psotka and Davison, 1993; Psotka and Calvert, 1994; Slater and Usoh, 1993; North, North and Coble, 1995a, 1995b, 1996a, 1996b, 1996c, 1997). Clearly the burdensome equipment and limited motion often stir feelings of claustrophobia to reduce the sense of immersion and open the way to simulation sickness (Kennedy, Lane, Lilienthal, Berbaum and Hettinger, 1992).

Immersion seems to be facilitated by the ability to control attention and focus on the new virtual reality to the exclusion of the real world. Being able to see parts of one's own body, even in cartoon form, adds to the experience. It also depends on a good visual imagination. People bring as much to the experience as the technology does (see Chapter Ten for more details). Those who undergo immersion in virtual reality environments experience a wide range of individual differences. The technological limitations are largely responsible; however, temperamental differences also account for different reactions. If the technological limitations of the burdensome equipment, shortage of detail, and slow computers were overcome, the individual differences would disappear. It is possible, however, that some difficulty might still exist which would destroy the voyagers' illusion. There is always the possibility that some voyagers will possess the knowledge that it is all virtual. Even a slight disturbance in the virtual reality environment, such as the a periodic heart-rate check, destroys the experience (Psotka and Calvert, 1994). Many of the limitations associated with the virtual reality experience are being reduced. Many voyagers or subjects are experiencing a powerful sense of direct engagement with the environment in spite of the currently limited capabilities available.

THE BENEFIT OF IMMERSION

Because of the excitement that surrounds the virtual reality environment, it has become a phenomenon that should be explored for potential use in education, training, psychotherapy, and other areas (Bricken and Byrne, 1993; North, North and Coble, 1995a, 1995b, 1996a, 1996b, 1996c, 1997). The motivation and mindful engagement (Salamon, Perkins and Globerson, 1991) that comes from this environment is not limited to its novelty, but also comes from the challenge, interactivity, realism, fantasy, cooperation and immersion that is a natural extension of the beneficial games and simulations it makes possible (Malone and Lepper, 1987). Part of this engagement comes from the thrill of new technologies; however, there is a more enduring and valuable component as well. Virtual reality is an empowerment technique that opens many new paths for learning (Pantelidis, 1993). Gay and Santiago (1994) report that high schools have effectively used virtual reality to stimulate interest in algebra, geometry, science, and the humanities. This was done by using only the crudest equipment.

Virtual reality provides a paradigm shift from previous interactive computer technologies. It permits all of the human senses, especially vision, the most communicative, to be used naturally. Virtual reality has the unique capacity to provide immersion in a combination of instructional games and simulations in its microworlds.

Virtual reality should not be seen as just another technology for human-computer interaction;it provides a fundamentally different mode of communication between computer and person, between symbolic form and mental representation and between collaborators in conceptual worlds. Virtual reality replaces interaction with immersion; it replaces the desktop metaphor with a world metaphor, and it replaces direct manipulation with symbiosis. The magnitude of these changes must be experienced to be understood.

Virtual reality augments learning with experience. This paradigm shift is a result of the compelling motivation of interaction with real time actions which can be interpreted symbolically and coordinated procedurally in body and mind. This coordination and communication can occur across distributed networks or with fictional places so that realistic and abstract spaces can be shared. In like manner, agents and objects can be represented in novel multidimensional formats in shared spaces to achieve a kind of multisensory integration that is akin to promote learning. If these uses of virtual reality for education and training are to be fulfilled, there is a great need to acquire more knowledge about the benefits and drawbacks of virtual reality and an even greater need for more advances in the technology of immersion (Durlach, Aviles, Pew, DiZio and Zeltzer 1992). If we are to know how best to use virtual reality in the mix of media and technologies available for instruction, we must create a principled path of research to discover the unique strengths and benefits of immersion for learning and in-struction.

Immersion and Visual Perspective

The most direct and compelling benefit that immersion offers to the cognitive interpretation of the world is a reduction in conceptual load because of the simplifying directness of perception of the virtual world (North, North and Coble, 1995a, 1995b, 1996a, 1996b, 1996c, 1997; Rothbaum, Hodges, Kooper, Opdyke, Williford and North, 1995a, 1995b). In most interaction with simulations, pictures, photographs, and line drawing representations, a human observer automatically constructs a virtual self, a viewpoint that enters the space of the drawing as if a human observer were there (Kubovy, 1986). Only very rarely is this virtual self and the real self in the same perspective location (Psotka, Davison and Lewis, 1993). It acts to make the experience less direct and reduces the cognitive resources available to carry out problem solving and mental representation of other issues.

Immersion and Field of View (FOV)

The accurate location of one's sense of self (one's egocenter) in a geometric space is of critical importance for immersion. Furness (1993) and Howlett (1990) report that immersion is only experienced when the field of view (FOV) is greater than 60 degrees or at least in the 60 to 90 degree FOV range. The theoretical rationale for this is not completely understood nor are there theoretical frameworks for one to follow in order to understand this phenomenon. The question is also important when dealing with simulation or motion sickness. Immersion environments are notorious for producing motion sickness. An inaccurate location of virtual egocenters may be implicated in this noxious effect. This effect may be related to the nonlinear compression of 140 degrees into an 18 or 45 degree FOV. This distortion effect needs to be investigated separately to determine how sensitive viewers are to determine FOV and compression-based distortions, pincushioning, and barrelling. Relationships with self-motion studies which deal with vection are also strongly dependent on FOV with larger fields that are more powerful for inducing optokinetic vection effects (Wertheim and Mesland, 1993; Wolpert, 1990). A key variable is the quality of immersion and the accuracy of self-localization. Informal comments by users of immersion environments have yielded many explanations for the number of errors in self-localization. Recently Psotka and Lewis (1994) discovered that the most verifiable sense of involvement in virtual reality comes with the widest possible FOV projection, even if the display is much smaller. They also discovered that judgments of distance in a virtual space are markedly non-linear when the field of view is less than 70 degrees.

Based on current technological limitations and due to the seamless nature of immersion and self localization, the task of designing a virtual reality appears to be difficult. Furthermore, it is impossible to create a wide FOV and HMD display at a reasonable cost. However, there are psychological components that offset this difficulty. Because adaptation to the distortions of a virtual reality environment is relatively easy (Dolezal, 1982), errors in self location diminish rapidly. Therefore the voyager is able to forget the real world and his place in it quickly. This permits the voyager in virtual reality to deal only with her location in virtual reality, and eliminates the burden of having to maintain her location in the virtual reality and the real world. In spite of the fact that the virtual world design is still flawed, learners should benefit from the singular sense of self in the virtual reality.

VIEWPOINT MANIPULATION

A clear indication of the present and potential implications for the uses of virtual reality research is that it is possible to manipulate the apparent location of one's virtual egocenter in many complex and mutually interacting ways. We do not understand how this is to be done, nor can we develop a clear cut training procedure, control mechanism, or process for communicating the results and possibilities this research holds. The artists of the Renaissance and Chinese landscape art offer some interesting clues about possibilities. Consider for instance Michelangelo's Last Judgment. In this stunning representation there is a grand conceptual unity of action encompassing huge areas of space with masses of saved humanity struggling upwards on the left, and the damned ricocheting down on the right. In the center, there is a massive stillness. What is dramatically unique about this conception is that there is no unique viewpoint portrayed by the artist. Every creature is at the center of the visual field, and yet, the artist was able to subtly unify the whole without the dominating constraint of a unique point of view. How has he done this? In part, he has created local areas of fixed viewpoint, so that the central figure creates peripheral views of the surrounding figures. Without this device the figures would all be flat, as if seen from infinity. Yet, he must have distorted the projection so that the surrounding figures are not as peripheral as they would have been with a true isomorphic projection. He may have gotten the inspiration for this piece from the dozens of larger panels that he created throughout the chapel. Each of the other pieces has a central viewpoint; he must have conceptually, if not physically, merged all of them throughout the chapel. In any event, the Last Judgement itself is unified by projection and by thematic constraints that affect projection in complex ways. It is not clear how a computer model of this image ought to be carried out. No modelling system can combine the multiple viewpoints and integrate them pleasingly and intuitively the way Michelangelo did. However, there is much that can be learned from close observation and study of Michelangelo's work. Instead of the strictly projective view of dataspaces, as cities and rooms, that we currently have, we might be able to lay out dataspaces that give equal emphasis to more distant and proximal areas, similar to a Chinese landscape. Clearly there are many potential uses for such a distortion of virtual space that range from command and control to communication and training.

VIRTUAL REALITY AND MOTION PLATFORMS

Visual information is not sufficient for immersion. Another key ingredient of immersion is accurate vestibular information that is synchronized with the cognitive motion plans and visual changes as the head turns, nods, or accelerates. If visual information were sufficient, there would be no need for head mounted displays. In like manner, motion is very important to the effectiveness of immersion in virtual reality. There is no explanation for the fact that motion platforms are not necessary for effective training. Also there is no training data that supports the use of motion-based simulators (Boldovici, 1993).

There may be many reasons to explain the missing data. One explanation is that motion may not help in some cases and because experimental techniques to determine the benefits of motion are missing or are inadequate. This is in sharp contrast to virtual reality experiences where motion is critical to immersion and the accurate and immediate recall of the location of novel objects (Pausch, Shackleford and Proffitt, 1993). Without the correlation of motion with visual change, the central and defining feature of virtual reality, presence or immersion is absent. In virtual reality environments, a person has to generate the motion to create the feeling of presence. In most current applications, you have to move your head, or turn your body. Based on this experience, it may be appropriate to infer that motion platforms may be needed when the virtual reality is not a first-person immersion or when it is a vehicle-based immersive environment, like SIMNET (a tank training virtual reality). Kinaesthetic stimuli are so important in virtual reality that it may be more appropriate to call upon virtual reality kinaesthetic visualization to emphasize the multimodal, dual nature of the immersive experience.

There is almost something magical about the way kinaesthetic and proprioceptive cues of turning one's head, correlated with visual changes, create this immersive experience. In virtual reality simulations, the contrast between a tracked display and an ordinary stationary display is like night and day. Without the kinesthetic and vestibular sensations that tracking the viewer's motion correlates with visual change, the images remain a dynamic movie of a tour through an environment. It is barely possible for most people to build a model of the environment in this untracked mode. By adding tracking and kinesthetic visualization, a powerful Gestalt is created out of the frames of experience. This Gestalt then surrounds and fills the space around a viewer in a complete mental model of the environment that is very useful for orientation, memory of locations, and navigation in general.

As we look around our environment, this kind of unification of a mosaic of images that we get as we move through our surroundings goes on effortlessly all the time. This unification is a very useful and powerful process that helps us react quickly to important features around us. Immersion is dependent on this process even though we do not understand how it works or what its limitations are.

Motion Cues

Motion cues provide a powerful support for grouping visual images seamlessly. Without them, our cognitive processes cannot understand the space around us. This is an important new implication of motion cuing that virtual reality makes obvious. It underscores the importance of motion platforms for simulators and the possibility of providing a way of showing a transfer of training benefit that is real, large, and worth the cost. Virtual reality makes it clear that motion platforms can be useful when we need spatial knowledge and when we need to remember where things are when they are out of sight.

One fruitful paradigm that has been identified for research to uncover visual vestibular interactions is called "cognitive tracking." In "cognitive tracking," instead of having an automated tracking device monitor head motion, subjects were asked to "play camera" and pretend that they are the camera and move the head mounted display in synchrony with changing video displays. The result was that it became clear that accurate synchrony of spatial motion of the head with changing visual perspectives results in improved immersion. Even when it is cognitively clear, there is no causal relation between head motion and changes in the visual display. Although past research has shown minimal benefit from the use of motion platforms in training, there are many reasons to explain why this benefit could not be found (Boldovici, 1993). The results of experiments in virtual reality shed a new light on the importance of motion in building a better sense of situational awareness.

TRANSFER OF LEARNING

Several early studies emphasized the potential use of virtual reality technologies for training, and the transfer from virtual reality experience to real world experience (Durlach, Aviles, Pew, DiZio and Zeltzer, 1992; Schlager, Boman, Piantanida and Stephenson, 1992). Recently, empirical data has been collected on the relative success of virtual reality in terms of instructional effectiveness, as well as the transfer of skill to the real world. For instance, Regian, Shebilske and Monk (1992) showed that people can learn to perform certain tasks from virtual environments (e.g., console operations, and large-scale spatial navigation). Also, knowledge and skill acquired in a virtual reality have been shown to transfer to performance in the real world. Regian, Shebilske and Monk (1993) found that: (a) virtual reality console operations training can transfer/facilitate real world console operations performance, and (b) virtual reality spatial navigation training successfully transfers to real-world spatial navigation. This finding is corroborated and amplified by Goldberg (1994). In contrast to these findings, however, those reported by Kozak, Hancock, Arthur and Chrysler (1993) showed no evidence for the transfer of a "pick and place" task from virtual reality to the real world. However, the criterion task used in that study was too easy and resulted in inclusive data.

In spite of the relatively poor fidelity and interface currently available in virtual reality technology, there is some evidence of its efficiency as a serious training/learning environment. For instance, the virtual reality environment has the potential to enhance new behaviors learned during the treatment for psychological disorders.

Goldberg (1994) reports on experiments at USARI Simulator Systems Research Unit (Moshell, Blau, Knerr, Lampton and Bliss, 1993) that show the value of tracked displays for learning to navigate through a complex building. In their experiment, subjects studied route directions and photographs of landmarks with or without a map of the building. They rehearsed in the building with a HMD and the model or with verbal directions. They were tested with actual traversals of the building. The real building produced fewer wrong turns (1.1) than the virtual model (3.3); however, both were significantly better than the verbal rehearsals (9.2). The virtual environment was almost as effective as the real building for learning route information.

In the area of psychology, the innovative research by North and North (1994); North, North and Coble (1995a, 1995b, 1996a, 1996b, 1996c, 1997) and a few other researchers have shown empirically that the clients with different phobias can, under virtual reality, learn a new adaptive behavior that was transferred to the real world situations.

CREATING THE VIRTUAL WORLD

Several approaches to creating virtual reality worlds are briefly covered in this section. The most common method is the use of head-mounted displays with a tracking sensor that reacts to the user's head movement, allowing participants to experience the virtual world from a self-viewpoint. This configuration can be complemented with additional interaction devices which offer participants almost full immersion.

The CAVE (Cave Automatic Virtual Environment) is a research project at the University of Illinois in Chicago, created by Tomas DeFontaine, which offers a full immersion system. The CAVE uses rear projection screens in a 10X10X10 foot cube that allows up to ten participants to become fully immersed in the virtual world. Only one participant in the group can control the virtual world by using a variety of input devices while other participants are passive observers. All participants wear stereoscopic shutter glasses to view the virtual world in three dimensional display.

Desktop virtual reality, on the other hand, uses the computer screen as a window through which the participants can view and interact with the virtual world. Although the desktop virtual reality system uses variety, input devices and special position tracking devices, this type of virtual reality system does not provide full immersion.

In projection virtual reality, participants can view images of themselves interacting with the virtual world in real time. The "Blu-Screen" process used in motion pictures and television (e.g., map projects in television weather reports) is utilized in the virtual reality project. Basically, the video camera image of the participant is combined with the images of the virtual world. The image is projected onto a large screen in front of the participant. This arrangement allows the participant to see herself navigating within the virtual world.

AUGMENTED REALITY

Augmented reality is a technology that uses see-through head-mounted displays that superimpose computer generated graphics over objects of the real world which, in turn, enhances an operator's perceptions of the real world. The see-through head mounted display may be made up of several technologies, which include: miniature cathode ray tubes (CRT), light emitting diodes (LED), or liquid crystal displays (LCD) which are derivatives of earlier head-up displays developed by the military. Military pilots use the head-up displays which permit them to see the weapons target data and other information while they are navigating through the real world. Position tracking sensors are used to overlay the graphics onto real world objects by using the position of the operator's head to track the object of interest in the real world. However, there are several problems that should be researched with the aid of augmented technology. In the area of alignment accuracy, the augmented reality technology is very promising. Current and future applications of augmented reality will be discussed in Chapter Eleven.

SHARED VIRTUAL REALITY

The virtual reality experience, which permits participants to be physically located in different places, can be shared by a group. The group participants would be able to interact with each other as well as objects in the shared virtual world. For example, in SIMNET, soldiers in tanks and aircraft simulators from different military bases can engage in a shared world to simulate battlefield exercises.

AFFORDABILITY

Recently, the cost of a virtual reality system has dropped drastically from 100 thousand dollars to less than 10 thousand dollars. The cost reduction has made it possible for our project to obtain a productive system which has been used effectively in our pilot studies of VRT. As reported by *CyberEdge Journal* in the January 1996 issue, this price reduction is a major milestone in virtual reality technology. The current price range will allow more researchers to conduct research that a few years ago was limited to only a few large corporations, government agencies, and universities.

Early virtual reality systems were only programming environments for researchers to conduct their research. However, today several software companies provide integrated and coherent systems for creating many different kind of virtual worlds. These programs are available to anyone who would like to explore virtual reality applications in their own field of expertise. A few of these integrated systems are available by VREAM, Inc.; Division, Inc.; SENSE8 Corporation; and Superscape, Ltd, just to name a few. With the explosion of PC computers, many of these companies are actively developing virtual reality software for PC users.

The most impressive virtual reality software development package is provided by VREAM, Inc. which has been providing support for our innovative virtual reality therapy as well as our other active research projects. In this section, we provide a brief description of the VREAM software. An integrative virtual reality system for use in the VRT that costs about ten thousands dollars can be obtained from a company in Atlanta for research purposes only (for more information you may contact the first named author of this book).

VIRTUAL REALITY DEVELOPMENT SYSTEM

As was mentioned earlier, there are several inexpensive virtual reality software packages on the market that can be utilized by researchers to conduct experiments in this exciting field. The VREAM virtual reality development system was helpful to us in building most of our innovative pilot virtual worlds. An overview of this system is provided below.

The VREAM software is easy to use and learn. It is basically a program-less environment for a low-end computer platform. The Windows version of the VREAM is called VRCreator and utilizes state of the art algorithms which will be constituting and leading the next generation of virtual reality software development.

The VREAM includes all of the software required to create, enter, and interact with complete virtual worlds on a standard personal computer (such as a Pentium based computer). The VREAM system allows the user to interact with virtual worlds by using inexpensive PC hardware, including a joystick, mouse, and keyboard, or by using higher-end virtual reality hardware, including head-mounted displays, 3D tracking systems, 3D mice, and gloves.

The VREAM system enables complete virtual worlds to be created using a window, mouse-driven, graphical user interface. Virtual worlds may be created by drawing the objects that comprise the virtual world. The attributes, structure, and interactivity of that world may then be defined by using the options available from the pull-down-menu structure. This allows virtual worlds to be created without the need to write complex computer programs. However, the VREAM system combines this ease of use with a great deal of power and flexibility. A completely scripted language is available in the VREAM system. This enables the user to directly access all of the capabilities of the VREAM system and to fully develop virtual reality applications.

FIGURE 1. A picture of a subject, accompanied by therapists (Dr. Max North and Professor Sarah North), getting immersed in a virtual world wearing a tracked head-mounted display.

CHAPTER 4

❖   ❖   ❖

VRT in the Treatment of Agoraphobia

This chapter is devoted to a landmark event: the first known extensive, controlled study to document the effectiveness of virtual reality therapy as a new modality for the treatment of psychological disorders. Because of the importance of this pioneering research, a reprint of a paper in the journal *Presence: Teleoperators and Virtual Environments*, Volume 5, No. 4, 1996, makes up the entire chapter. The multimedia version of this report can be found in The *International Journal of Virtual Reality*, Volume 1, No. 2, 1995. An abstract may be found in the October 1995 issue of the *CyberEdge Journal*.

Effectiveness of Virtual Environment Desensitization in the Treatment of Agoraphobia

Max North, Ph.D., Sarah North, M.S.D. and Joseph Coble, Ph.D.
Virtual Reality Technology Laboratory
Clark Atlanta University

ABSTRACT

The primary purpose of this study was to investigate effectiveness of the virtual environment technology in the area of psychotherapy.

Consequently, this study investigated the effectiveness of virtual environment desensitization (VED) in the treatment of agoraphobia (fear of being in places or situations from which escape might be difficult or embarrassing). Sixty undergraduate college students served as subjects. Thirty subjects served in the experimental group and the other thirty served as a control group. Subjects' degree of fear/anxiety was measured using two instruments, the Attitude Towards Agoraphobia Questionnaire (ATAQ) and the Subjective Units of Disturbance (SUD) Scale. Only subjects in the experimental group were exposed to the VED treatment. The virtual environment desensitization was effective in the treatment of subjects with agoraphobia (experimental group). The scores of the control group did not change significantly, while both ATAQ and SUD scores decreased significantly for the experimental group. The average SUD scores of the experimental group decreased steadily across sessions, indicating steady improvement from treatment. It is hoped that this research will be a first step toward the utilization of virtual environment technology in providing more effective, economical, and confidential treatment of psychological disorders.

INTRODUCTION

Agoraphobia is defined as fear of being in places or situations from which escape might be difficult or embarrassing (American Psychiatric Association, 1994). Agoraphobic fears typically lead to a pervasive avoidance of a situation such as being in a crowd of people; staying in a line; traveling in an automobile, bus, or airplane; or being on a bridge or in an elevator. People with this disorder suffer from marked distress about having the fear, and experience significant behavioral difficulties. These behavioral dysfunctions cause interference with normal routines and/or with interpersonal relationships that can result in significant distress. In the field of mental health, agoraphobia is one of the most prevalent anxiety disorders, accounting for approximately 60% of all phobic disorders in community populations (Michelson, Mavissakalian and Marchione, 1985). Behavioral therapy often includes graded exposure of the subject to anxiety-producing stimuli (Systematic Desensitization). These stimuli are commonly generated either through the subject's imagination or in vivo (subject experiences real situations).

In utilizing systematic desensitization, research reviews demonstrate that many clients appear to have difficulty imagining the prescribed anxiety-evoking scene (Schneider, 1982; Michelson, Mavissakalian and Marchione, 1985). They also express strong aversion to experiencing real situations (Pendleton and Higgins, 1983; James, Hampton, May and Larsen, 1983). This avoidance may be a learned behavior that lowers the anxiety of clients, thus reducing their public embarrassment.

Virtual environment is a technology that enables users to enter computer-generated worlds and interface with them through sight, sound, and touch. Virtual environment differs from traditional displays in that computer graphics and various display and input technologies are integrated to give the user a sense of presence or immersion in the virtual environment (Held and Durlach, 1992; Bryson, 1992; Sheridan, 1992). Virtual environment offers a new human-computer interaction paradigm in which users are no longer simply external observers of data or images on a computer screen. They are active participants within a computer-generated three-dimensional virtual world. Virtual environment is also called virtual reality, telepresence, artificial worlds, cyberspace, or multisensory input/output.

Virtual environment technology may be utilized to overcome some of the difficulties inherent in the traditional treatment of agoraphobia. Virtual environment, like current imaginal and in vivo modalities, can generate stimuli that could be utilized in desensitization therapy. Like systematic desensitization therapy, virtual environment desensitization (VED) therapy can provide stimuli for clients who have difficulty in imagining scenes and/or are too phobic to experience real situations. Unlike in vivo systematic desensitization, VED can be performed within the privacy of a room, thus avoiding public embarrassment and violation of client confidentiality. Similar to lens-assisted in vivo (Schneider, 1982), virtual environment can generate stimuli of much greater magnitude than standard in vivo techniques. Since VED is under client control, it appears safer than in vivo desensitization and at the same time more realistic than imaginal desensitization. Finally, VED adds the advantage of greater efficiency and economy in delivering the equivalent of in vivo systematic desensitization within the counselor's office.

As far as we know, the idea of using virtual reality technology to combat psychological disorders was first conceived within the Human-

Computer Interaction Group at Clark Atlanta University on November 1992. Since then, we have successfully conducted the first known pilot studies in the use of virtual environment technologies in the treatment of specific phobias: fear of flying (North and North, 1994), fear of heights (Williford, Hodges, North and North, 1993; Rothbaum, Hodges, Opdyke, Kooper, Williford and North, 1995a; North and North, 1996b), and fear of being in certain situations (such as a dark barn, an enclosed bridge over a river, and in the presence of an animal [a black cat] in a dark room) (North, North and Coble, 1995a). As of now, several other researchers have realized the potential of virtual reality in the treatment of psychological disorders. These contemporary research activities establish a new paradigm that appears to be attracting serious scientists from the computer science, psychology, and medical fields. The present study sought to extend the previous work to include more systematic study with a larger number of subjects and a wider range of virtual environments.

RESEARCH METHODOLOGY

Subjects

Subjects were 60 undergraduate male and female students at Clark Atlanta University who were suffering from agoraphobia and who voluntarily agreed to participate in the study. Subjects were recruited through questionnaires distributed to undergraduate students enrolled in core courses at Clark Atlanta University. The questionnaires contained items which screened students for agoraphobia according to DSM-IV (American Psychiatric Association, 1994) criteria and excluded subjects with a history of panic disorder. Additional screening criteria included in the questionnaire were symptom duration of at least one year and a strong motivation toward overcoming agoraphobia.

Measures

Subjects rated their maximum level of anxiety on a modified ten-point Attitude Towards Agoraphobia Questionnaire (ATAQ) (Abelson and

Curtis, 1989) and a modified eleven-point Subjective Units of Distur-bance (SUD) Scale (Wolpe, 1961). The ATAQ consists of six pairs of antonyms, each of which is rated on a scale from zero to ten. These sets of antonyms are good-bad, nice-awful, pleasant-unpleasant, safe-dangerous, non-threatening-threatening, and harmless-harmful. In the SUD, subjects simply rate their level of discomfort in a present or proposed situation on a scale from zero to ten. Subjects with scores of less than two or more than eight on the ATAQ and/or SUD were excluded from the study. Remaining subjects were randomly assigned to one of two groups: a virtual environment desensitization group (ex-perimental group) or a waiting list (control group). There were no significant mean differences between the two groups on pre-test scores on either instrument.

Procedure

Apparatus

The virtual environment system for this study consisted of a stereoscop-ic head-mounted display (CyberEye, General Reality Company), an electromagnetic head-tracker (Flock of Birds, Ascension Technology), and a data glove (Power Glove) worn by the subject for interacting with objects in the virtual environment. Interactive imagery was generated by software developed at the Human-Computer Interaction Group and Virtual Reality Technology Laboratory at Clark Atlanta University and the GVU (initial pilot study), executing on a Silicon Graphics Work-station and Pentium Personal Computer (VREAM Virtual Reality Development Software).

Virtual Environment Scenes

Several virtual environment scenes were created, as described by subjects and considering software limitations, for use in the therapy sessions. The VREAM software was used to create virtual environment scenes for this study.

- Series of Balconies Scene—consisted of four balconies attached to a tall building. The balconies were at ground level, second floor level (six meters), tenth floor level (thirty meters), and twentieth floor level (sixty meters), (Figure 1).
- Empty Room Scene—consisted of four walls, ceiling, and floor. The room was four by six meters in size, with only one door (entrance and exit). There were no windows or furniture in this room (Figure 2).
- Dark Barn Scene—consisted of a barn in an open field. The interior of the barn was black (simulating darkness). The barn had a wide door, so that subjects could exit the barn as quickly as they wished. There were several dark colored objects inside the barn (Figure 3).
- Dark Barn with a Black Cat Scene—A black cat was simulated within the dark barn. The black cat was placed on top of an object. The black cat was not visible from outside the barn. In order to see the black cat, the subject had to enter the barn and look to the right (Figure 4).
- Covered Bridge Scene—contained a bridge (ten meters high) that ran across a river and had walls on each side and a ceiling. There were two windows on each of the walls. Dark colors were used to simulate a closed environment (Figure 5).
- Elevator Scene—consisted of an open elevator (no walls or ceiling) located in the atrium of a 49-story hotel (Figure 6).
- Canyon with Series of Bridges Scene—contained three bridges of different heights spanning the canyon from one side to the other. A river ran through the bottom of the canyon. The bridges varied not only in height but also in apparent steadiness. The lowest two bridges (seven and fifty meters) appeared safe and solid. The highest bridge (eighty meters) was a rope bridge with widely spaced wooden slats as the flooring (Figure 7).
- Series of Balloons Scene—consisted of three hot-air balloons at different heights. The first balloon was at twenty meters height, the second balloon at thirty meters height, and the third balloon at forty meters height. There were a one-floor building and a four-floor building in the scene (Figure 8).

Experimental Protocols

Only subjects in the experimental group were exposed to the VED treatment. In the initial laboratory session, which lasted approximately 20 minutes per subject, the VED subjects were familiarized with the virtual environment equipment. During this session, VED subjects also eliminated any of the eight scenes described above which did not cause anxiety, and ranked the remaining scenes from least to most threatening. For the VED subjects' subsequent eight sessions, which were 15 minutes each for eight weeks (one session per week), individual virtual environment desensitization was conducted in a standard format. The first session began with the least threatening level of the subject's least threatening scene. The SUD (the subject simply rating his/her discomfort on a scale of zero to ten) was administered every five minutes. Subjects progressed systematically through each level of a scene, and then moved to their next most threatening scene. This progress was totally under the control of the subject, with the exception that if a subject's SUD score was two or less, the experimenter urged the subject to move up to the next level or next scene. Each session after the first began at the scene and level at which the subject's previous session ended. After eight weeks, a post-test of all subjects in experimental and control group was conducted to obtain ATAQ and SUD scores.

RESULTS

Means and standard deviations of ATAQ and SUD Pre-test and Post-test scores of experimental and control group subjects were calculated and may be seen in Table 1. The strong correspondence between scores on the two instruments provides a good validity check, since the tests both measure subjective discomfort on a 11-point scale, with the SUD being simply a rating of general discomfort, while the ATAQ measures discomfort on six emotional dimensions.

Comparisons of relevant sets of group means were performed using t-tests, and may be seen in Table 1. Here it may be seen that there were no significant differences between the pre-test scores of the two groups on either instrument, indicating that the two groups were well matched as to initial severity of discomfort. There were also no significant differences between the pre-test and post-test scores of the control group on either test, demonstrating that the severity of symptoms did not spontaneously change over the course of the experiment. Significant differences were found between the pre-test and post-test scores of the experimental group on both instruments, and between the post-test scores of the two groups on both tests. These means and t-test results indicate that the post-test scores of the experimental group were significantly lower than both their pre-test scores and the post-test scores of the control group, implying a reduction in agoraphobic symptoms as a result of the VED treatment.

Means and standard deviations were calculated for the SUD scores obtained during each treatment session for the experimental group, and may be seen in Table 2. The mean SUD scores of the experimental group decreased steadily from each session to the next, implying that the experimental group experienced habituation from repeated graded exposure to threatening virtual environments.

DISCUSSION

While this was a preliminary study and has definite limitations, it is an important step toward the possible treatment of phobic clinical patients using VED. The results indicated that VED was very effective in reducing self-reported anxiety of most members of the experimental group, whereas the control group did not demonstrate any significant change. Eighty percent of the experimental subjects experienced a reduction of over 50% in subjective discomfort according to both instruments used in this study.

We cannot explain why 20% of the subjects showed little or no reduction in discomfort according to one or both instruments, but we do have two hypotheses. The experimenters noted that many subjects commented on the high degree of reality they experienced in the virtual environments, but such comments were not universal. Also, while most subjects steadily moved to higher levels and more threatening scenes, there were some who changed levels or scenes only slowly or when urged to do so by the experimenters. Since the major focus of this study was simply to examine the effectiveness of VED, there were no specific measures of sense of presence, and detailed records of the number of levels and scenes viewed by each subject were not kept. Both sense of presence and motivation (as indicated by the rate of progress through different levels and scenes) will be measured in future studies.

It should also be noted that this study does not speak to the relative effectiveness of VED and conventional imaginal systematic desensitization, as the control group used in this study was simply a no-treatment group. We did not feel it prudent to incur the temporal and monetary costs of including an imaginal systematic desensitization (ISD) group until it was shown that VED was more effective than no treatment. Such an ISD group will be included in future work.

Although somewhat limited, the present results are definitely important. They attest to the sense of presence experienced by subjects in the virtual environment. The degree of anxiety and habituation observed would not have occurred if the subjects did not immerse in virtual environment. The relatively high SUD scores (where subjects simply rated their present subjective discomfort) obtained during early training sessions indicates that the anxiety levels of subjects were raised through exposure to the virtual environments; and the steady reduction in SUD scores across the training sessions indicates habituation (reduction in anxiety responses) as a result of the virtual environment exposure. While we do not expect clinicians to rush to purchase virtual reality hardware and software upon reading this study, these results are certainly promising. With further research, it is our belief that VED may well prove to be a cost- and time-effective alternative to the treatment of phobic disorders.

ACKNOWLEDGEMENTS

We thank the anonymous referees for their detailed comments, Dr. Nat Durlach for his professional support, and Derrick Nelson for help in modeling of the virtual scenes. This research project was sponsored by a grant from Boeing Computer Services (Virtual Systems Department), partially supported by U.S. Army Research Laboratory under contract number DAAL03-92-6-0377. The views contained in this document are those of the authors and should not be interpreted as representing the official policies of the U.S. Government, either expressed or implied.

TABLE 1. Means (and Standard Deviations) and comparison of mean of Pre-test and Post-test Scores of Experimental and Control Group Subjects on the Attitudes Toward Agoraphobia Questionnaire (ATAQ) and the Subjective Units of Disturbance scale (SUDs)

| | Experimental Group (Received Treatment) | | | | | | Control Group (Did Not Receive Treatment) | | | | | |
| | Baseline (N=30) | | After 8 Weeks (N=30) | | Analysis (df=58) | | Baseline (N=30) | | After 8 Weeks (N=30) | | Analysis (df=58) | |
Measure[a]	Mean	SD	Mean	SD	t	P	Mean	SD	Mean	SD	t	P
ATAQ	5.49	0.94	2.01	1.52	3.07	<0.05	5.21	0.54	5.76	0.63	0.38	<0.05
SUDs	5.24	0.70	2.04	1.40	2.96	<0.05	5.38	0.67	5.53	0.72	0.10	<0.05

[a] A higher rating indicates greater distress.

TABLE 2. Mean SUD Scores for Experimental Subjects for Individual Treatment Sessions

Treatment Session	SUD Scores for Experimental Subjects	
	Mean	SD
1	5.66	0.74
2	5.54	0.74
3	5.24	0.77
4	4.54	0.80
5	3.72	1.03
6	3.25	1.19
7	2.76	1.22
8	2.42	1.38

FIGURE 1. Series of balconies scene.

FIGURE 2. Empty room scene.

FIGURE 3. Dark barn scene.

FIGURE 4. Dark barn with a black cat scene.

FIGURE 5. Covered bridge scene.

FIGURE 6. Elevator scene.

FIGURE 7. Canyon with series of bridges scene.

FIGURE 8. Series of balloons scene.

CHAPTER 5

Effectiveness of VRT for Acrophobia

This chapter includes two independent research reports on using virtual reality technology to combat acrophobia (fear of heights). It begins with the first known controlled report which was the outcome of our collaborative initiative work with other universities in Georgia. This report is reprinted by permission of the *American Psychiatric Association* from *The American Journal of Psychiatry*, 152:4, pp. 626-28, April 1995 (Copyright 1995). The second report is on the first known extensive case study, conducted exclusively at CAU. The original report of this case study can be found in *the Journal of Medicine and Virtual Reality, Computers, Imagery, Photonics, and Robotic Applications*, Volume 1, No. 2, 1996, published by Virtual Reality Solutions, Inc., New York, New York. In addition, a news brief was included in the January 1996 issue of the *CyberEdge Journal*. Since VRT appears to be working very well with acrophobic patients, we are continuing our research in this area to better understand the nature of it, and to improve our knowledge of the sense of virtual presence, which is one of the major factors of VRT, as well as other virtual reality applications.

Effectiveness of Computer-Generated (Virtual Reality) Graded Exposure in The Treatment of Acrophobia

Barbara Olasov Rothbaum, Ph.D., Larry F. Hodges, Ph.D., Rob Kooper, I.R., Dan Opdyke, M.S., James S. Williford, M.D., and Max M. North, Ph.D.

Objective: The authors' goal was to examine the efficacy of computer-generated (virtual reality) graded exposure in the treatment of acrophobia (fear of heights). Method: Twenty college students with acrophobia were randomly assigned to virtual reality graded exposure treatment (N=12) or to a waiting-list comparison group (N=8). Seventeen students completed the study. Sessions were conducted individually over eight weeks. Outcome was assessed by using measures of anxiety, avoidance, attitudes, a and distress associated with exposure to heights before and after treatment. Results: Significant differences between the students who completed the virtual reality treatment (N=10) and those on the waiting list (N=7) were found on all measures. The treatment group was significantly improved after 8 weeks, but the comparison group was unchanged. Conclusion: The authors conclude that treatment with virtual reality graded exposure was successful in reducing fear of heights.

Behavioral therapy of acrophobia usually includes exposing the patient to anxiety-producing stimuli while allowing anxiety to attenuate (Abelson and Curtis, 1989; Williams et al, 1984). Since exposure to relevant stimuli usually requires leaving the therapist's office, it is important to identify alternatives to such exposure.One possible alternative to standard in vivo exposure may be computer-generated (virtual reality) graded exposure. Virtual reality integrates real-time computer graphics, body tracking devices, visual displays, and other sensory input devices to immerse a participant in a computer-generated virtual environment. Kijima and Hirose (unpublished 1993 paper) reported that virtual reality was used in Japan to simulate the sand play projective technique with autistic children. These authors presented no data, but they contended that the virtual reality sand play was useful. In a single case study (Rothbaum et al, 1995b), we found that treatment with virtual reality graded exposure was effective for reducing fear of heights.

To our knowledge, this report represents the first controlled study of virtual reality in the treatment of a psychological disorder. The purpose of this study was to examine the efficacy of a treatment for acrophobia by using virtual reality graded exposure treatment in a methodologically controlled design. Treatment with virtual reality graded exposure has the advantages of conducting time-consuming exposure therapy without the patient's leaving the office, potentially offering more control over exposure stimuli. Thus, it may offer a time- and cost-effective way to conduct exposure therapy.

METHOD

Four hundred seventy-eighty college students were screened for acrophobia. Twenty students who indicated substantial fear and avoidance of heights entered the study. Twelve were men, 18 were Caucasian, and their mean age was 20 years (SD=4); 17 of the 20 students completed the study. Students with concomitant panic disorder were excluded because wearing the virtual reality helmet might cause them distress.

Measures included the Acrophobia Questionnaire (Cohen, 1977), a screening questionnaire, the Attitude Towards Heights Questionnaire (adapted from the work of Abelson and Curtis 1989), and the Rating of Fear Questionnaire. The students given virtual reality treatment also rated their levels of subjective discomfort (range=0-100) every 5 minutes during exposure.

Hardware consisted of a head-mounted display and an electromagnetic sensor that was used to track the head and right hand so that the user could interact with objects in the virtual environment. Virtual reality hardware and software were integrated with a square platform (4 ft by 4 ft) surrounded by a railing. This platform aided exposure by giving the subject railing to hold an edge to approach, it also kept the subject within tracking range of the sensor. The hardware and software have been described in greater detail elsewhere (Hodges et al, 1994).

Originally, 31 students were randomly assigned to a treatment condition (virtual reality or waiting list) following screening for acrophobia. Twenty students (12 who had been assigned to virtual reality treatment and eight who had been assigned to the waiting list) attended the group pretreatment assessment. During the group pretreatment assessment the study was explained, informed consent was obtained, and baseline self-report scales were completed.

After the group pretreatment assessment, the 12 students in the treatment group received their first treatment session. At that time they were familiarized with the virtual reality equipment. After seven weekly sessions of virtual reality graded exposure (8 weeks after the group pretreatment assessment), they completed the same measures. The students in the waiting list condition completed the same measures after eight weeks with no treatment. Treatment and assessment were provided free of charge.

Individual virtual reality graded exposure treatment was conducted in seven weekly 35-45 minute sessions by an advanced clinical psychology graduate student (D.O.). The students spent as much time in each situation as they needed for their anxiety to decrease; each progressed at his or her own pace. The therapist simultaneously viewed on a video monitor all of the virtual environments in which the students were interacting and commented appropriately, as would be expected for conventional exposure.

The following virtual environments were encountered: 1) three footbridges that were 7, 50, and 80 meters above water; the two lower bridges could be viewed from the highest bridge and added to the sensation of height, 2) four outdoor balconies with railings that were on the ground, second, 10th, and 20th floors, and 3) one glass elevator simulating the elevator at the Atlanta Marriott Marquis convention hotel, rising 49 floors, up to 147 meters at the top; the subject controlled the movement of the elevator by using three "buttons."

The effect of virtual reality treatment on the measures was tested by using the change by treatment interaction term from a repeated measures analysis of variance computed with the BMDP 5V computer program (Dixon, 1992) by using the REML algorithm and compound symmetry covariance structure. The maximum likelihood estimation procedure used by the computer program results in a chi-square statistic rather than the usual F statistic. This procedure was chosen because it did not require the exclusion of subjects for whom values were missing. The chi-square for the interaction of change by group assesses differences in the amount of improvement between groups.

RESULTS

No pretreatment differences were detected between the group of students given treatment and those in the waiting list condition on any measures or demographic variables. The results and analyses of the assessments before and after treatment are presented in Table 1 [Rothbaum et al]. As can be seen, measures of anxiety, avoidance, distress (Rating of Fear Questionnaire), and all attitudes toward heights decreased significantly from the pretreatment assessment to the posttreatment assessment for the virtual reality graded exposure treatment group but not for the waiting list comparison group. Examination of the individual attitude ratings revealed that the means on all items were below 4.0 at posttreatment assessment for the treatment group, indicating positive attitudes on the semantic differential scale. In contrast, all attitudes were negative for the waiting list comparison group at posttreatment assessment. The mean rating of subjective discomfort in each session decreased steadily across sessions, indicating habituation.

Seven of the 10 students who completed the virtual reality graded exposure treatment exposed themselves to height situations in vivo between treatment sessions, although they were not specifically instructed to do so. These exposures appeared to be meaningful, including riding 72 floors in a glass elevator and intentionally parking on the top floor of a parking deck close to the edge rather than in the center of the ground floor.

CONCLUSION

In this controlled study of the application of virtual reality to the treatment of a psychological disorder, we found that students treated with virtual reality graded exposure experienced reductions in self-reported anxiety and avoidance of heights and improvements in attitudes toward heights and that students in a waiting list comparison group did not evidence any change. Although the students in the current study group were not patients seeking treatment, our results are comparable to those of Cohen (1977). The pretreatment anxiety and avoidance scores for Cohen's subjects, who were acrophobic patients seeking treatment, were 60.64 and 13.83, respectively, which are comparable to the pre-treatment scores of the students in the present study. The anxiety and avoidance raw scores of Cohen's subjects decreased by 28.6 and 6.7, respectively, after treatment with systematic desensitization; the scores of our students treated with virtual reality graded exposure decreased by 37.3 and 13.3, respectively.

In addition to our selected study group, other limitations of this study included the absence of a treatment comparison group, especially subjects given standard exposure treatment, the absence of follow-up data, and no formal assessment of phobic avoidance. Despite these limitations, our findings provide support for the use of virtual reality graded exposure in the treatment of height phobias. Virtual reality also appears applicable in the treatment of other anxiety disorders in which exposure-based treatments are recommended. The reasonable applications and limits of therapy assisted by virtual reality must be established.

Virtual Reality Psychotherapy

Max M. North, Ph.D., and Sarah M. North, M.S.D.
Virtual Reality Technology Laboratory
Clark Atlanta University

ABSTRACT

Acrophobia can be defined as fear of height which is classified under agoraphobia, fear of being in places or situations from which escape might be difficult (or embarrassing). Imaginal and in vivo systematic desensitization (SD) have been effective in the treatment of agoraphobia (e.g., acrophobia). Current computer and display technology allows the creation of virtual environments (VE); VE can provide an important intermediate step between imaginal systematic desensitization and self-directed maintenance in vivo SD. This unique and in-depth case study demonstrates the effectiveness of virtual environment desensitization (VED) in the treatment of acrophobia of a subject who suffered of fear of heights. The results indicated a significant habituation of subject on anxiety symptoms as well as avoidance of subject phobic situation.

INTRODUCTION

Acrophobia is classified as a specific phobia in the Diagnostic and Statistical Manual of Mental Disorders (American Psychiatric Association 1994). People having this disorder suffer from marked distress about having the fear or from significant behavior difficulties. Behavior dysfunction involves interference with normal routine or with interpersonal relationships. There have been relatively few publications of controlled research on the therapy of acrophobia. Behavioral therapy has included exposing the subject to anxiety producing stimuli. These stimuli are generated through a variety of modalities including imaginal (subject generates stimulus via imagination) and in vivo (subject experiences the real world) (Schneider, 1982). In addition to current in vivo and imaginal modalities, virtual environments (VE) can also generate stimuli that will be utilized in desensitization therapy. Like in vivo therapy, virtual environment desensitization (VED) therapy will provide stimuli for patients who cannot imagine well. VED will be used as an intermediate step in preparing patients for maintenance therapy involving self-directed in vivo exposure.

As in vivo SD provides stimuli for the patient who cannot imagine well, VE based on stereoscopic head-mounted displays with head-tracking will produce visual and auditory stimuli. Unlike the in vivo technique VE will allow therapist-assisted SD within the confines of a clinician's office, thus avoiding public embarrassment and violation of patient confidentiality. VE adds the advantage of greater control over graded exposure stimulus parameters and the ability to isolate which virtual stimulus parameters are essential in generating a phobic response, as well as greater efficiency and economy in delivering the equivalent of in vivo exposure within the therapist's office.

Virtual Environments offer a new human-computer interaction paradigm in which users are no longer simply external observers of data or images on a computer screen but are active participants within a computer-generated three-dimensional virtual word. Virtual environments differ from traditional displays in that computer graphics and various display and input technologies are integrated to give the user a sense of presence or immersion in the virtual environment (Sheridan, 1992). There are several approaches to creating virtual environments. Head-mounted displays consist of separate display screens for each eye that are attached to the head along with some type of display optics and a head-tracking device (Teitel, 1990). Time-multiplexed CRT displays present a stereoscopic image by alternating right-and left-eye view of a scene on a CRT. The image is viewed through a shutter system that occludes the left eye when the right-eye image is on the screen and vice versa (Hodges, 1992). Time-multiplexed projection displays operate similarly to time-multiplexed CRTs, but the images are projected onto one or more large screens (Cruz-Neira et al, 1992). Projection and CRT stereoscopic displays may or may not also incorporate head-tracking.

Virtual environments also provide special techniques that allow users to interact with virtual spaces. Current techniques include the use of special gloves that track hand and finger positions so that the user can grasp virtual objects, six-degrees-of-freedom mouse and navigation devices, and locomotive devices such as treadmills, bicycles, or "flying" chairs that allow users to move about in the environment (Bryson, 1992).

The idea of using virtual reality technology to combat psychological disorders was first conceived within the Human-Computer Interaction Group at Clark Atlanta University on November 1992. Since then, we have successfully conducted the first known pilot studies in the use of virtual reality technologies in the treatment of agoraphobia (North and North, 1994, North, North and Coble, 1995a, 1995b). This includes the investigation of the use of virtual reality for specific phobias: Fear of heights, fear of flying, and fear of being in certain situations (such as a dark barn, an enclosed bridge over a river, and in the presence of an animal [a black cat] in a dark room). Evidently several other researchers have realized the potential of virtual reality in the treatment of psychological disorders. These contemporary research activities establish a new paradigm that appears to be attracting serious scientists from the computer science, psychology, and medical fields.

METHODOLOGY

Case History

A 42-year-old married man who conducts research at Clark Atlanta University sought treatment for fear of heights. The preliminary analysis based on data collected from SUD (Subjective Units of Disturbance scale) (Wolpe 1961) and subject having symptoms limited to acrophobia and consistent with the diagnosis of specific phobia revealed the existence of fear of heights. The client's anxiety and avoidance behavior were interfering with his normal life activities. He was unable to go to his office on the 4th floor. Neither using an elevator nor taking the stairs was comfortable. The subject was recruited through questionnaires distributed to employees in the science and technology center of Clark Atlanta University. The questionnaires contained items which screened subjects for acrophobia according to DSM-IV (American Psychiatric Association 1994) criteria and excluded subjects with a history of panic disorders. Additional screening criteria included in the questionnaire were symptom duration of at least one year and a strong motivation toward overcoming acrophobia. Subject rated his maximum level of anxiety on a modified eleven-point SUD. In the SUD, subjects simply rate their level of discomfort in present or proposed situations on a scale from zero to ten.

Apparatus

The virtual environment system for this study consists of a stereoscopic head-mounted display (CyberEye, General Reality Company), an electromagnetic head-tracker (Flock of Birds, Ascension Technology), and a data glove (Power Glove) worn by the user for interacting with objects in the virtual environment. We have configured a virtual environment PC-based system that costs less than $10,000, including the tracking device, head-mounted display, and several other interaction devices generally affordable by general practitioners.

Virtual Environment Scenes

The VREAM Virtual Reality Development Software Package and Libraries were used to create virtual reality scenes for this study. We have created an outdoor balcony scene with railing at four heights: Ground floor (0 meter), second floor (6 meters), 5th floor (15 meters), and 15th floor (45 meters). Several streets, buildings, and a bridge on a river appear in the scene (see Figure 1).

Treatment Procedure

After we obtaining informed consent, subject was asked to rank order a list of the acrophobic situations according to the degree of anxiety arousal. During the VED subject's first session, he was familiarized with the VE technology through several demonstrations. For the subject's subsequent eight sessions, which were between 15 and 28 minutes each, individual VED therapy was conducted in a standard format. The first session began with the least threatening level which was at the ground level near a bridge crossing a river in the middle of a simulated downtown. The SUD was administrated periodically every two to five minutes. Subject progressed systematically through each level of the virtual scene. This progress was totally under the control of the subject, with the exception that if the subject's SUD score was zero, the experimenter urged the subject to move up to the next level of the scene. At one month post treatment, subject was asked to complete a eleven-point rating scale (including degrees for worsening symptoms) rating the degree to which his aerophobia symptoms have changed since pre-treatment test (SUD).

RESULTS AND CONCLUSION

SUD rating measured the degree of which the subject was effected by VED. In VED therapy the subject's anxiety usually increased as he was exposed to more threatening situations (e.g., higher balcony), and decreased as he remained in each situation (a normal psychological effect in human beings). Table 1 [North and North] and Figure 2 illustrate the SUD rating which varied with time and the height location of the subject during the eight VED therapy sessions. Subject in the virtual reality scene appeared to be feeling fully immersed. This was evidenced by his rating of the sense of presence in virtual world and absence of the sense of presence in physical world and his comments during and after each session. Some of the comments:

"I am really there!"
"I am afraid to fall down."
"My palms are sweaty."
"I feel weak in my knees."

Symptoms Experienced During VED Therapy

Subject experienced a number of physical anxiety symptoms during the VED therapy sessions. These symptoms included sweaty palms, loss of balance, weakness in the knees. Table 1 [North and North] and Figure 2 also illustrate how SUD ratings varied with balcony level (height) and time during the eight VED sessions. Apparently, Table 1 [North and North] and Figure 2 demonstrate the increase of anxiety at the beginning of each level and session and show steady reduction after the subject spent some time in the virtual scene. This pattern also appeared in our pilot studies with other phobic situations and subjects. The subject definitely became immersed in the virtual scene to the extend that he had to grasp a hand rail in the laboratory to avoid falling in virtual environment and maintaining his balance (see subject's comments at different level and time in Table 1 [North and North]).

Typically, longer exposure to virtual environments causes simulator sickness which arises from discrepancies between visual and kinetic perceptions; it is similar to the motion sickness (Pausch et al, 1992). Extended exposure to virtual reality also may cause physical and psychological injury. Therefore, therapy sessions were limited to 15-28 minutes, in an effort to avoid any physical and emotional discomfort for the subject.

DISCUSSION

Similar to our previous innovative pilot studies (first reported controlled studies) using virtual reality for treatment of agoraphobia, the results of this case study indicated that VED was very effective in reducing self-reported anxiety. The subject of this study had a fear of flying as well as fear of heights. At this time he is being treated with VED for fear of flying, specifically fear of flying over rivers, lakes, and oceans. At this time, subject can comfortably go about his normal life activities and is dealing with acrophobia more realistically than before.

While conducting the treatment, we discovered that the subject's anxiety level increased whenever he was placed near a river or lack (in virtual environment). The fact of his being more anxious while close to water situations was not apparent to the subject before this experiment. Thus, the VED appeared not only to reduce the anxiety level of subject, but also evoked the subject's deeper fear memory structure and resulted in discovering and better understanding of his phobic situation. In another words, VED resulted in deeper introspection of the subject's disorder.

Although somewhat limited, the present results including the pilot studies are very impressive. They attest to the sense of presence experienced by subject(s) in virtual environments. The degree of anxiety and habituation observed would not have occurred if the subject had not been immersed in the virtual environment scene. The high SUD scores obtained during the treatment sessions indicate that the anxiety level of subjects are raised through exposure to the virtual environments; and the steady reduction in SUD across the treatment sessions indicates habituation.

TABLE 1 [Rothbaum et al]. Anxiety Scores of College Students With Acrophobia Treated or Not Treated With Virtual Reality Graded Exposure Before and After Treatment

Measure [a]	Received Treatment				Did Not Receive Treatment				Analysis	
	Baseline (N=12)		After 8 Weeks (N=10)		Baseline (N=8)		After 8 Weeks (N=7)		X^2 (df=1)	p
	Mean	SD	Mean	SD	Mean	SD	Mean	SD		
Acrophobia Questionnaire										
Anxiety	54.4	24.4	17.1	11.7	54.3	11.4	46.1	15.3	14.79	<0.0001
Avoidance	16.5	10.8	3.2	2.7	15.8	7.8	16.7	7.7	14.10	<0.0002
Total	70.9	34.4	20.3	13.2	70.0	17.7	62.9	19.1	16.14	<0.0001
Attitudes Towards Heights Questionnaire										
Bad	6.6	1.7	2.9	1.8	5.0	2.1	5.6	0.5	18.91	<0.0001
Awful	6.0	1.5	2.9	1.6	5.3	2.3	6.0	0.6	14.69	<0.0001
Unpleasant	5.7	3.1	3.5	1.7	6.0	2.4	7.0	1.5	4.43	<0.04
Dangerous	7.4	2.5	3.0	2.3	6.5	2.6	7.3	1.6	14.71	<0.0001
Threat	7.0	2.0	3.0	1.9	6.6	2.7	6.9	1.9	11.76	<0.0006
Harmful	6.8	2.0	2.7	1.8	6.1	2.0	6.7	1.8	18.31	<0.0001
Total	39.5	9.8	18.0	10.3	35.5	12.6	39.4	6.4	18.14	<0.0001
Rating of Fear Questionnaire	4.1	1.8	1.9	1.3	3.5	1.3	3.3	1.5	9.33	<0.002

[a] A higher rating indicates greater distress.

72

TABLE 1 [North and North]. Comments (including physical and emotional symptoms) provided by the subject during the eight VED sessions.

VED Scene Level Session	Min	SUD	Comments
Ground level (0 meter) Session one	1	5	Searches for a hand rail to hold on to. "I feel like falling down when looking up to the top of building."
	5	4	"My whole body shakes." (Will not let go of hand rail)."
	10	3	(Will not let go of hand rail).
	12	3	
	15	2	
	17	1	Notices that has fear of being near a river. (Will not let go of hand rail).
	20	0	
Second floor (6 meter) Session two	0	8	Grasps for hand rail. "I do not like it, I do not feel comfortable at all.
	5	6	I may fall down into the river!"
	7	3	
	8	2	
	10	4	Moved closer to the middle of bridge.
	15	0	
Second floor (on river) Session three	1	8	"I cannot look down to see the river, I am falling down into river."
	5	6	Holds to the hand rail firmly.
	11	4	
	15	0	
Second floor (on river) Session four	0	8	"It feels like the bridge is vibrating".
	5	5	
	10	6	
	15	5	"My palm is sweating."
	20	4	Sweaty palms continues. "This hand rails help me not to fall into the river."
	25	5	
	26	3	
	27	1	
	28	0	

73

TABLE 1 [North and North]. Continued

VED Scene Level Session	Min	SUD	Comments
Fifth floor (15 meters)	0	10	"Can I close my eyes?"
Session five	4	8	
	8	6	
	10	4	
	12	7	"I do not like to stand on this floor."
	15	3	"It feels like being on seventh floor."
	17	1	"Now I can look around."
	20	0	
Fifth floor	2	3	While looking down to the river, he feels dizzy and falling down.
Session six	5	6	"I am feeling dizzy."
	8	5	
	10	4	
	15	6	"Still feeling dizzy."
	18	3	
	21	0	
Fifteenth floor (45 meters)	0	7	
Session seven	7	5	"I can hear music coming from the river and birds singing."
	10	5	"It is windy here.
	14	5	"It looks higher when I look down."
	16	3	
	18	1	"I feel comfortable now."
	19	0	
Fifteenth floor	0	5	"I feel like I am exactly on the fiftieth floor."
Session eight	5	4	"I feel dizzy when I look down."
	7	3	"I can hear the music coming from the river."
	10	1	"I feel comfortable at this height."

FIGURE 1. Series of balconies scene showing several street buildings, and a bridge on a river.

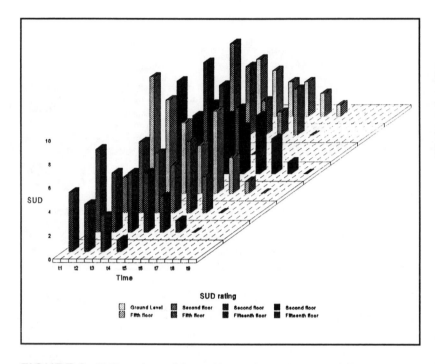

FIGURE 2. SUD rating of the subject with respect to different balcony level and time (t1..t9) for all the eight VED sessions.

CHAPTER 6

❖ ❖ ❖

VRT Combats Fear of Flying

The research report in this chapter is the first known in-depth case study of the effectiveness of VRT in treating fear of flying. It was conducted at CAU during the summer of 1995. The report is reprinted from the Journal of *Presence: Teleoperators and Virtual Environments*, Volume 6, No. 1, 1997 (in print), MIT Press. An extended abstract also may be found in the *Human Factors and Ergonomics '96* conference proceedings, and a short abstract in the *American Journal of Psychiatry*, 1996, and the January 1996 issue of the *CyberEdge Journal*. It was a panel presentation at the *Medicine Meets Virtual Reality IV* conference in San Diego in January 1996. A second case study of the use of virtual reality exposure therapy in the treatment of fear of flying was reported briefly at the same conference by Hodges, et al. In this report, a virtual airplane was used for exposure therapy of a 42-year-old female subject who suffered from fear of flying. Although the researchers reported that the virtual reality exposure therapy was effective, they did not present extensive data at that time and they did not provide us with more details of their project for inclusion in this chapter.

Virtual Environment Psychotherapy:
A Case Study of Fear of Flying Disorder

Max M. North, Ph.D., Sarah M. North, M.S.D., and
Joseph R. Coble, Ph.D.
Virtual Reality Technology Laboratory
Clark Atlanta University

ABSTRACT

Fear of flying is a common disorder affecting a large number of people globally. Current computer and display technology allows the creation of virtual environment scenes which can be utilized for specific psychological disorders. This case study demonstrates the effectiveness of virtual environment desensitization (VED) in the treatment of a subject who suffered from fear of flying. The subject, accompanied by a virtual therapist, was placed in the cockpit of a virtual helicopter and flown over a simulated city for five sessions. The VED treatment resulted in both a significant reduction of anxiety symptoms and the ability to face the phobic situations in the real world.

INTRODUCTION

Fear of flying is classified as a specific phobia under agoraphobia according to the criteria of the Diagnostic and Statistical Manual of Mental Disorders (American Psychiatric Association, 1994). People who have this disorder suffer from various symptoms caused by fear and often resulting in significant behavior difficulties. Behavior dysfunction involves interference with normal routine, professional or interpersonal relationships. According to an internal report by the Boeing Company, over 25 million people in the United States are afraid to fly and 20 percent of the people who have to fly on a regular basis rely on sedatives or alcohol during flights to deal with the fear. Behavioral therapy has included exposing the subject to anxiety producing stimuli (systematic desensitization therapy). These stimuli are generated through a variety of modalities including imaginal (subject generates stimulus via imagination) and in vivo (subject experiences the real world) (Schneider, 1982). In addition to current imaginal and in vivo modalities, virtual environments can also generate stimuli that will be utilized in desensitization therapy. Virtual Environment Desensitization (VED) will be used as an intermediate step in preparing patients for maintenance therapy involving self-directed in vivo exposure.

As in vivo, VED provides direct stimuli for the patient. Virtual environments employ the use of stereoscopic head-mounted displays with a head-tracking unit to produce visual and auditory stimuli (Bryson, 1992; Cruz-Neira, Sandin, DeFanti, Kenyon, and Hart, 1992; Sheridan, 1992). Unlike the in vivo technique, VED will allow therapist-assisted systematic desensitization within the confines of a clinician's office. This arrangement will eliminate public embarrassment and violation of patient confidentiality. VED also has the advantage of providing greater control over graded exposure stimulus parameters and the ability to isolate which virtual stimulus parameters are essential in generating a phobic response, as well as greater efficiency and economy in delivering the equivalent of in vivo exposure within the therapist's office.

To the best of our knowledge, we have conducted the first controlled pilot studies in the use of virtual environments technology in the treatment of phobias (North and North, 1994; North, North, and Coble, 1995a; North and North, 1996b; North, North, and Coble 1996a; North, North, and Coble, 1996c). The present work sought to extend the previous works to investigate an in-depth case study of a subject who suffered from fear of flying.

METHODOLOGY

Subject

A 42-year-old married man who conducts research at Clark Atlanta University sought treatment for the fear of flying. The preliminary analysis based on data collected from SUD (Subjective Units of Disturbance scale) (Wolpe, 1961) and the fact that the subject had symptoms limited to and consistent with the diagnosis of specific phobia (acrophobia and fear of flying) (American Psychiatric Association, 1994) confirmed a diagnosis of fear of flying. The subject's anxiety and avoidance behavior were interfering with his normal activities. For example, he was unable to travel to professional conferences, visit relatives or take a vacation by air. The subject was recruited through phobia screening questionnaires distributed to employees housed in the science and technology center of the Clark Atlanta University. The subject was first diagnosed and treated for acrophobia, fear of height, in the summer of 1995.

Apparatus

The virtual environment system for this study consisted of a stereoscopic head-mounted display (CyberEye, General Reality Company) which provides crisp, undistorted images equivalent to a 7-foot-wide TV screen placed 12 feet away. The unit had a visual field of view of 22.5 degrees horizontal X 16.8 degrees vertical and an audio frequency response of 20hz-20khz. This was combined with an electromagnetic 6D multi-receiver/transmitter head-tracking device (Flock of Birds, Ascension Technology) with an update rate of up to 144 measurements per second and a data glove (Power Glove) worn by the user for interacting with objects in the virtual environment. The VREAM Virtual Reality Development Software Package and Libraries were used to create a virtual reality scene for this study. This configuration is a virtual reality PC-based system that costs less than $10,000, including the tracking device, head-mounted display, and several other interaction devices, a cost well within the means of average practitioners.

Virtual Environment Components

The Virtual City scene

An area within 40-kilometer radius was created, the city of Atlanta at the center. The scene contained major highways, major roads, two large lakes, and the Chattahoochee River. The most easily distinguished skyscrapers in downtown Atlanta could be recognized in this scene.

Several farm lands and houses were placed in the suburban areas. Airports, subdivisions, and other landmarks were observable while subjects flew over the virtual city. A portion of the virtual city is shown in Figure 1.

The virtual Apache Helicopter

The flying was accomplished by a simulated McDonnell Douglas AH-64A Apache helicopter. A helicopter was chosen instead of a commercial airliner for two major reasons. First, the helicopter provided a more intense visual stimulus, with a panoramic view rather than the small windows in the passenger compartment of commercial airliners. Second, the helicopter provided much more precise control of movement than would be realistically possible with a fixed-wing aircraft. The helicopter could travel at a wide variety of speeds, hover, move backward, and even change altitude without moving forward—all movements which cannot be performed by fixed-wing aircraft.

The Apache cockpit was roughly simulated for the subject and his virtual therapist who was placed in the back seat. A simulated audio (helicopter's engine sound) was also a part of the environment. For a more realistic effect, a vibration apparatus was placed under the physical cockpit. The visual, audio and tactile cues were all synchronized to provide the subject with a maximum sense of virtual presence. The Apache was designed to take off from the simulated Atlanta Hartsfield International Airport, fly over the city at a low altitude for approximately 30 minutes, return to Atlanta Hartsfield Airport, and land.

Virtual Therapist

A model of a therapist was created and placed on the co-pilot seat behind the subject's seat. The virtual therapist wore a simulated flight helmet and dark flight glasses. The virtual therapist scenario allowed the physical world therapist to communicate with the subject in the virtual world without drawing the subject's attention back and forth from the virtual world to the physical world. This arrangement allowed the subject to be totally involved in the virtual world at all times, which ultimately provided an opportunity for a deeper and uninterrupted sense of immersion. It also allowed the subject to communicate with the virtual therapist who had no distinguishing features. As a result, the subject could imagine the virtual therapist to be anyone he wished, such as a friend, parent, mentor, or any other person of significance in the subject's life. To increase interaction with the virtual therapist, the voice of the physical world therapist was channelled through the earphones worn by the subject. This allowed the physical world therapist to be in the virtual world with the subject. The same arrangement is being tested for multi-participant virtual reality which can be achieved through a local or global computer network.

Treatment Procedure

The subject of this study had some familiarity with the VED procedure, since he had received treatment for his acrophobia (fear of heights) disorder as a subject in a previous study. During the subject's five sessions in the current study, which lasted 20 to 30 minutes each, individual VED therapy was conducted in a standard format—similar to customary desensitization in systematically moving from less threatening to more threatening scenes, with the rate of progression among scenes controlled by the subject; differing from regular systematic desensitization in not including any formal desensitization training. The first session began with the least challenging level which involved sitting in a virtual AH6-64A Apache cockpit at the virtual Atlanta Hartsfield International Airport. During the next four sessions, more challenging situations included flying over the virtual city and eventually over the virtual river and a virtual lake. The SUD was administrated every two to five minutes. With the SUD the subject is simply asked to rate his/her level of anxiety/fear on an 11-point scale ranging from 0 (totally relaxed) to 10 (blind panic) (Wolpe, 1961). The subject progressed systematically through each level of the virtual scene. The progression was totally under the control of the subject except that when the subject's SUD score was zero, the experimenter urged the subject to move to the next level.

RESULTS AND CONCLUSION

The SUD ratings measured the degree to which the subject was affected by VED. In VED therapy the subject's anxiety usually increased as he was exposed to more challenging situations (e.g., flying over a river or lake), and decreased as the time in that situation was increased. Tables 1 (a-e) illustrate SUD ratings which varied with time and level during the five VED therapy sessions. The subject in the virtual reality scene appeared to be feeling fully immersed. This was evidenced by his rating of the sense of presence in the virtual world and the absence of the sense of presence in the physical world. Some of the comments made by the subject while in the virtual world were: "It feels like being in a real helicopter!" "I feel like I'm really flying!" "It feels like that helicopter is crashing into the lake!" "I am really there!" This is merely a preliminary study with a single subject, and the data presented here are all subjective. Nevertheless, the consistent decline in SUD scores throughout each session, as well as the increase in SUD scores when moving to more challenging scenes, are worthy of note. Still more noteworthy is the fact that since treatment the subject has taken several actual flights, and reported experiencing considerably less anxiety than was the case prior to the VED therapy.

Symptoms Experienced During VED Therapy

The subject experienced a number of physical and emotional anxiety-related symptoms during the VED therapy sessions. These symptoms included sweaty palms, loss of balance, weakness in the knees, etc. Tables 1 (a-e) also illustrate how the SUD ratings varied with level and time during the five VED sessions. Tables 1 (a-e) demonstrate the increase in anxiety at the beginning of each session and shows the steady reduction of anxiety after the subject spent time in the virtual scene. This pattern also appeared in the previous study in which the subject was treated for height phobia. There the subject became immersed in the virtual scene to the extent that he had to hold on to a hand rail in the laboratory to maintain his balance as he interacted in the virtual world. See Tables 1 (a-e) for the subject's comments at different levels and times.

VED sessions were limited to 20-30 minutes each, because it has been shown that longer exposures to virtual environments cause simulator sickness which comes from discrepancies between visual and kinetic perceptions, similar to motion sickness (Pausch, Crea and Conway, 1992). Also, the extended exposure to virtual reality may cause physical and psychological damage to the subject. The limited treatment times proved to be safe and comfortable, as the subject in this study reported no physical or emotional side effects.

DISCUSSION

Similar to our first reported controlled study to use virtual reality for the treatment of agoraphobia, the results of this case study indicted that VED was effective in reducing self-reported anxiety. At this time the subject can comfortably take a flight. Since the termination of the treatment, he has taken several flights to professional conferences and reported that more comfort and reduced symptoms than those experienced prior to the VED treatment.

While conducting the treatments with this subject, especially the treatment for the fear of heights, it was discovered that the subject's anxiety level increased whenever he was placed near a river or lake in the virtual world. The fact that he became more anxious while close to water was not apparent to the subject before this experiment. The VED appeared not only to reduce the anxiety level of the subject but also to evoke a specific memory of a previous experience in the subject's life, resulting in a better understanding of his phobic situation. In other words, VED provided insight into the etiology of the subject's disorder.

Although rather limited, the present results are quite promising. These results attest to the sense of presence experienced by the subject in the virtual environments. The degree of anxiety and habituation observed in the subject would not have been expected if the subject had not become immersed in the virtual environment scene. The high SUD scores obtained during the treatment sessions strongly implied that the anxiety level of the subject was raised through exposure to the virtual environment scenes; and the steady reduction in SUD within the treatment sessions seemed to demonstrate habituation. Most importantly, the positive effects of VED treatment did appear to transfer to actual commercial flight situations.

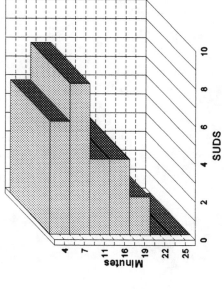

TABLE 1 - a. Session one: Sitting in the cockpit of the Apache with engine running

"I feel like I am in a real helicopter!" 4

Grasps for the hand rail to hold on 7

"I need to hold on to the rail." 11

"I do not feel comfortable at all!" 16

Will not let go of the handrail.................19

"I feel much better now." 22

"The simulation is great!" 25

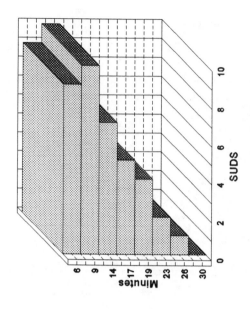

TABLE 1 - b. Session two: Flying over the virtual city

Feeling dizzy...6

"I do not like this at all!"...9

Sweaty Palms, uncomfortable when looking down.......14

"My palms are really sweaty!".....................................17

"I feel like I am flying over Atlanta!".........................19

Feels calmer...23

Getting more comfortable..26

"I feel O.K."...30

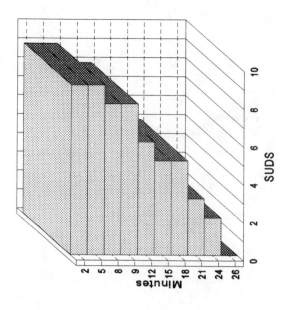

TABLE 1 - c. Session three: Continuing to fly over the virtual city

"I feel very nervous!"	.2
Feeling dizzy again	.5
"I am very scared!"	.8
Sweaty palms	.9
"I am feeling a little better"	.12
"I am much more comfortable now!"	.15
Getting more comfortable	.18
Enjoying the flight	.21
More relaxed now	.24
"I feel very comfortable and relaxed now"	.26

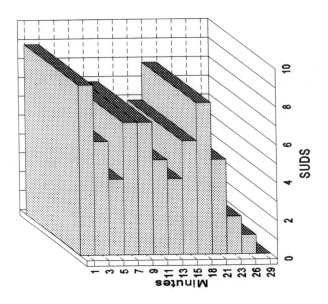

TABLE 1- d. Session four: Flying over the river and the lake

Feeling uneasy and nervous...1
Having trouble with breathing..3
"I feel better now"...5
flying over the river...7
"I am scared!"...9
"I can see the river, I am riding over it!"..................11
"It is really scary to ride over the river!"................13
Scared, sweaty palms, holding to the hand rail......15
"It feels like the helicopter is crashing into the river!"....16
"I feel like I am flying over the Atlantic ocean"......21
(away from the river), enjoying the ride now...........23
"I feel O.K. while passing the river now!"................26
Feels comfortable..29

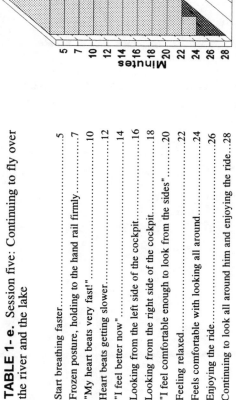

TABLE 1- e. Session five: Continuing to fly over the river and the lake

Start breathing faster.	5
Frozen posture, holding to the hand rail firmly.	7
"My heart beats very fast!"	10
Heart beats getting slower.	12
"I feel better now"	14
Looking from the left side of the cockpit.	16
Looking from the right side of the cockpit.	18
"I feel comfortable enough to look from the sides".	20
Feeling relaxed.	22
Feels comfortable with looking all around.	24
Enjoying the ride.	26
Continuing to look all around him and enjoying the ride.	28

FIGURE 1. A portion of the virtual city is shown from the cockpit of a virtual Apache helicopter.

❖   ❖   ❖

Related Reports of VRT

This chapter covers two preliminary reports of the use of virtual reality technology to assist patients in dealing with their psychological disorders. These reports support our discovery of and research findings concerning VRT. Both reports were presented at *Medicine Meets Virtual Reality IV* conference in San Diego, January 1996. The first report is a new approach to treating patients with eating disorders. A multimedia version of this report may be found in the *International Journal of Virtual Reality*, Volume 2, No. 2, 1996. The second report is a virtual reality application to help autistic children. It is partially reprinted here from the *Journal of Presence: Teleoperators and Virtual Environments*, Volume 5, No. 4, 1996, MIT press.

Virtual Reality and Body Experience: A New Approach to the Treatment of Eating Disorders

Giuseppe Riva, Ph.D.
Applied Technology for Psychology Laboratory, Intra, Italy

ABSTRACT

Eating disorders, which are one of the most common pathologies of the Occidental society, have long been associated with alterations in the perceptual/cognitive representations of the body. In fact, a large number of studies have highlighted the fact that the perception of one's own body and the experiences associated with it represent one of the key problems of anorexic, bulimic and obese subjects, the effects of which have a strong influence on therapy effects: severe body representation disturbance is predictive of treatment failure. However, the treatment of body experience problems is not well defined. Two methods are currently in use: the first is a cognitive/behavioral approach aimed at influencing patients' feelings of dissatisfaction; the second is a visual/motorial approach with the aim of influencing the level of bodily awareness. The Virtual Environment for Body Image Modification (VEBIM), a set of tasks aimed at treating body image, tries to integrate these two therapeutical approaches within an immersive virtual environment. This choice would not only make it possible to intervene simultaneously on all of the forms of bodily representations, but also to use the psycho-physiological effects provoked on the body by the virtual experience for therapeutical purposes. The paper describes the VEBIM theoretical approach and its characteristics; also it presents a study on a preliminary sample (60 normal subjects) to test the efficacy of this approach.

INTRODUCTION

The perceptual world created by our senses and our mind is so functional a representation of the physical world that most people live out their lives without ever suspecting that contact with the physical world is mediate. The physical world, including our body, is not given directly in our experience but is inferred through observation and critical reasoning. This means that, in everyday life, the body as a representation/image/idea plays an important and often under-rated role. It is interesting to note that these representations are not limited to visual "images" (i.e., pictures in one's head of one's body) but comprise the schema of all sensory input internally and externally derived-lived experiences processed and represented within a maturing psychic apparatus.

Body Schema and Body Image

This "virtual body" has been the subject of a number of studies which, however, often make reference to concepts and theories different one from the other: "body percept", "body image", "body concept", "body schema" and "body values". Recently, an attempt has been made to incorporate all of the forms of perceptive/cognitive representation of the human body within two fundamental concepts (Gallagher, 1986, 1995; Fisher, 1990): body schema and body image. According to Head (1926), the body schema is a model/representation of one's own body that constitutes a standard against which postures and body movements are judged. This representation can be considered the result of comparisons and integrations at the cortical level of past sensory experiences (postural, tactile, visual, kinesthetic and vestibular) with current sensations. This gives rise to an almost completely unconscious "plastic" reference model that makes it possible to move easily in space and to recognize the parts of one's own body in all situations. If the body schema can be considered a perceptual model of the body, the body image is a cognitive/social/emotional model. In fact, body image is not only a cognitive construction but also a reflection of wishes, emotional attitudes and interactions with others. According to Schilder (1950), the body image can be defined as "the picture of our own body which we form in our mind, that is to say, the way in which the body appears to ourselves" (p. 11).

Expanding on Schilder's idea, Allamani et al (1990) refer to body image as "a complex psychological organization which develops through the bodily experience of an individual and affects both the schema of behavior and a fundamental nucleus of self-image" (p.121). The circular interaction among behaviors, emotions and cognitions we find in body image can be explained by the rational-emotive model (Ellis, 1962; Freedman, 1990): X, an activating event (e.g., wearing a skirt), leads to Y, a bridging thought and self statement (e.g., "I'm too big"), which triggers Z, a conditioned emotional response (e.g., disgust, anxiety). In this way X, the activating event, generates new cognitions which then induce new feeling (e.g., "I'm fat") and behavior (e.g., dieting). Behavioral disturbances may thus be both a cause and an effect of faulty thinking.

How Body Schema Can Affect Body Image

Gallagher (1995) analyzed recent psychological studies on the relationship between body image and body schema. His report stated that performances of the body schema may place constraints on intentional consciousness. More in particular, the studies indicated that changes in various aspects of body schema have an effect on the way subjects perceive their own bodies, that is, changes in body schema lead to changes in body images. More generally, changes in body schema also affect spatial perception and perception of objects. Here are some of the examples reported in the paper:

Exercise, dance, and some other practices that affect motility and the postural schema have an effect on the emotive evaluation of one's own body image (Adame et al 1991, Dasch 1978, Davis and Cowles 1991, Skrinar et al 1986). In these studies, subjects who through exercise improve in neuromuscular coordination, strength, and endurance, or experience increased coordination, balance, agility, and improved posture, gain a perception of body competence and achieve a higher degree of satisfaction with their own bodies. Thus changes in body schema associated with exercise alter the way that subjects emotionally relate to and perceive their bodies.

Changes in muscular schemata correlate with changes in the subject's bodily awareness and perceptual awareness of the environment (Ruggieri et al, 1983; Sabatini, Ruggieri and Milizia 1984). These studies also suggest that unconscious adjustments of the body schema allow the subject to direct attention to external rather than internal stimuli. More generally, to the extent that the body schema makes its pre-noetic adaptations to the environment and remains in the perceptual background, cognitive attention can be focused elsewhere in any variety of intentions.

Retardation in the development of the body schema caused, for example, by an absence of early crawling experience has a negative effect on the development of spatial perception. Studies by Joseph Campos and his colleagues have demonstrated that crawling and locomotor experience in infants have an effect on the perception and evaluation of spatial heights (Campos, Bertenthal and Kermoian 1992).

Several studies indicate that proprioceptive adjustments of the body schema help to resolve perceptual conflicts. Adaptation in the realm of visual experience involves changes in proprioceptive information. For example, perceptually adapting to 180 degree rotation of the retinal image is facilitated by "changes in the position sense for various parts of the body" (Harris, 1965, p. 419).

Experimental studies indicate that there is a "close linkage between eye posture or movements and the spatial organization of the whole-body posture" (Roll and Roll 1988, 159). Thus vibration of extraocular eye muscles results in body sways and shifts in balance. But also, vibration-induced proprioceptive patterns that change the posture of the whole body are interpreted as changes in the perceived environment. It follows that alterations in proprioceptive information, information closely connected to the organization of the body schema, lead to changes in visual perception. In all of these cases, changes or distortions introduced at the level of the body schema result in changes or distortions in intentional consciousness. But this simply reflects the general rule. In all cases, performances of the body schema influence intentionality. They operate as constraining and enabling factors that limit and define the possibilities of intentional consciousness.

Definition of Body Experience Disturbance

Body experience disturbance has been used by a wide variety of researchers and clinicians to designate a great number of phenomena with little or no overlapping characteristics (Thompson, 1992). For instance, the phrase neuropsychological deficits (anosognosia) has been used to refer to phantom limb syndrome, and the psychodynamic concept of "body boundary" (Thompson, 1990). In this paper we will focus exclusively on a physical appearance related definition that is quite broad body experience disturbance is any form of affective, cognitive, behavioral, or perceptual disturbance that is directly concerned with an aspect of physical appearance.

Body experiences have a long and storied association with eating and weight related problems (Stunkard and Mendelson, 1961; Bruch, 1962, 1973; Garfinkel and Garner, 1982; Barrios et al, 1989; Rosen, 1990; Thompson, 1990; Valtolina et al, 1994; Thompson, 1995). Bruch

(1962) articulated the integral role of body experience in the development, maintenance, and treatment of anorexia nervosa. In later years, researchers also agreed that body experience was a central factor in bulimia nervosa (American Psychiatric Association,1994; Thompson, Berland, Linton, and Weinsier, 1986). Finally, although often ignored as a feature of obesity (see Thompson, 1990), Stunkard and Burt (1967) demonstrated almost 30 years ago the importance of body experience to an understanding of individuals with excessive weight. One index of the importance of body experience disturbance involves its relevance to agreed-on clinical disorders. The Diagnostic and Statistical Manual of Mental Disorders IV (American Psychiatric Association, 1994) contains a body image criterion that is required for the diagnosis of anorexia nervosa or bulimia nervosa. It has also been suggested that, when there is psychological co-morbidity with obesity, it may be strongly due to problematic body experience issues (Thompson, 1992).

Today, researchers and clinicians agree that including an assessment and evaluation of body experience disturbance is crucial to any treatment program targeting obesity or eating disorders. Some studies concerning the efficacy of the cognitive-behavioral treatment of anorexia have indicated that patients who make a larger overestimate of their own bodily dimensions (Casper et al, 1979) or who are more pleased with their own physical appearance (Vandereycken et al, 1988) gain less weight after a period of treatment. Furthermore, among those who manage to reach their target weight, post-treatment weight loss correlates directly with the way in which patients perceive their own size (Button, 1986). Also in the treatment of bulimic subjects, body experience has been shown to play an important role in assessing the outcome of treatment. In particular, the degree of satisfaction that patients have in relation to their bodies has been shown to be related both to a reduction in bulimic behavior and to subsequent relapses.

In contrast to the great number of publications on body image, only a few papers focus on the treatment of a disturbed body image in eating disorders. In general, two direct and specific approaches can be distinguished: a cognitive/behavioral approach aimed at influencing patients' feelings of dissatisfaction with different parts of their bodies by means of individual interviews, relaxation and imaginative techniques (Butter and Cash, 1987), and a visual/motorial approach which makes use of video recordings of particular gestures and movements with the aim of influencing the level of bodily awareness (Wooley and Wooley, 1985).

Virtual reality is a medium that is defined in terms of its effects on basic perception and higher order psychological processes (Ellis, Kaiser and Grunwald, 1991). Steuer (1992) defines virtual reality in terms of human experience as "a real or simulated environment in which a perceiver experiences telepresence". In fact, virtual reality creates a sense of personal presence by simulating as closely as possible the range and intensity of stimuli that human senses detect in perceiving the natural world. In immersion virtual reality, you know you are "there" because the virtual world responds like the real world to your body and head movements (Heeter, 1992).

A New Challenge

An interesting possibility could be the integration of the two methods (cognitive-behavioral and visual-motorial) commonly used in the treatment of body experience disturbances within a virtual environment. In particular we tried to integrate them using the virtual environment in the same way as images in the well-known method of guided imagery (Leuner, 1969).According to this method the therapist, after introducing a selected image, encourages the patient to associate to it in pictures, rather than in word, and to give a detailed description of them. It's Leuner's belief that the imagery evokes intense latent feelings that are relevant to the patient's problems. Guided imagery has been found to be a powerful tool in treatment approach ranging from psychoanalytic therapy (Reyker, 1977) to behaviorism (Wolpe, 1958). A choice of this type would not only make it possible to evoke latent feelings, but also to use the psycho-physiological effects provoked by the experience for therapeutical purposes. Is well known that in practically all virtual reality systems, the human operator's normal sensorimotor loops is altered by the presence of distortions, time delays and noise in the system. Such alterations, that are introduced unintentionally and usually degrade performance, affect body perceptions, too. The somesthetic system has a proprioceptive subsystem that senses the body's internal state, such the position of limbs and joints and the tension of the muscles and tendons. Mismatches between the signals from the proprioceptive system and the external signals of a virtual environment alter body perceptions and can cause discomfort or simulator sickness (Sadowsky and Massof, 1994). In a recent study, Cioffi (1993) analyzed these effects and found that in virtual reality the self-perception of one's own body undergoes profound changes that are similar to those achieved in the 1960s by many psychologists in their studies of perceptual distortion. In particular, about 40% of the subjects felt as if they had "de-materialized" or as if they were in the absence of gravity; 44% of the men and 60% of the women claimed not to feel their bodies. Perceptual distortions, leading to a few seconds of instability and a mild sense of confusion, were also observed in the period immediately following the virtual experience. Such effects, attributable to the reorganizational and reconstructive mechanisms necessary to adapt the subjects to the qualitatively distorted world of virtual reality, could be of great help during the course of a therapy aimed at influencing the way the body is experienced, because they lead to a greater awareness of the perceptual and sensory/motorial processes associated with them. As we saw before, changes in various aspects of body schema have an effect on the way subjects perceive their own bodies, that is, changes in body schema lead to changes in body images. When a particular event or stimulus violates the information present in the body schema (as occurs during a virtual experience), the information itself becomes accessible at a conscious level (Baars, 1988). This facilitates the process of modification and, by means of the mediation of the self (which tries to integrate and maintain the consistency of the different representations of the body), also makes it possible to influence body image.

SYSTEM DESIGN AND IMPLEMENTATION

The Virtual Environment for Body Image Modification—VEBIM—was developed using a Thunder 100/C virtual reality system by Virtual Sys of Milano-Italy. The Thunder 100/C is a Pentium based immersive virtual reality system including an HMD subsystem and a two-button joystick-type motion input device.

The Display System

A head mounted display with 52i H and 41i V field of view provided the visual display. The HMD displays 624 lines of 210 pixel to each eye and uses LCD technology (two active matrix color LCDs). A Logitech 3D Mouse provided head tracking. In this research we did not use a stereoscopic display. Previous researches regard stereoscopy as important because it provides the user with a good cue of depth (Barham and McAllister, 1991). However, the refresh rate of graphics decreases by 50% for the need of two different images for each eye. Consequently, we decided against implementing a stereoscopic display. To compensate for the lack of depth cue, we included perspective cues (light and shade, relative size, textural gradient, interposition and motion parallax) in the virtual environment (Dolecek, 1994).

Motion Input System

The data glove-type motion input device is very common in virtual environments for its ability of sensing many degrees of freedom simultaneously. However the operator is also frequently confused by the difficulty in correctly using it, especially when there is a time delay contained in the feed-back loop. To provide a easy way of motion in VEBIM we used an infrared two-button joystick-type input device: pressing the upper button the operator moves forward, pressing the lower button the operator moves backwards. The direction of the movement is given by the rotation of operator's head.

THE VIRTUAL ENVIRONMENT

VEBIM is a 6-zone virtual environment developed using SENSE8 World Toolkit for Windows. VEBIM consists of two parts (zones 1-2 and zones 3-4-5-6). The first two zones are designed both to give the subject a minimum level of skill in perceiving, moving through and manipulating objects in virtual reality, and to focus his attention on eating and food choice. The next four zones are designed to modify the body experience of the subject integrating the therapeutical methods used by Butter and Cash (1987) and Wooley and Wooley (1985). Both at the beginning of zone 3 and at the end of zone 6 the subject is submitted to a series of procedures/tasks aimed at assessing his body experience. Zone 1: In this zone the subject familiarizes with the appropriate control device, the head mounted display and how to recognize collisions. To move into the next zone the subject has to weigh himself touching a virtual balance. Zone 2a and 2b: these zones contains a kitchen (2a) and an office (2b). The subject can move between them and interact with the objects. Some of them are foods that the subject can take and "eat". To move into the next zone the subject has to weigh himself again (his starting weight will be modified according to the actions made and the food eaten). Zone 3: this zone consists of four corridors whose walls show images of female and male models. Zone 4: this is a room furnished with a large mirror. Standing by it the subject can look at his real body (previously digitized using a video camera). Zone 5: this zone consists of a long corridor ending with a room containing four doors of different dimensions. The subject can move into the last zone only choosing the door corresponding exactly to his width and height. Zone 6: this is a large room whose leading walls (north and south) show the body of the subject. The first image is a static one (real body) and cannot be changed, while the second one (ideal body) can be changed by the subject according to his own desire (by using a morphing-like system).

A PRELIMINARY STUDY

Until now some problems have existed with virtual reality. There are anecdotal reports that immersive virtual reality can lead to symptoms similar to motion sickness symptoms. Visually induced motion sickness is a syndrome that occasionally occurs when physically stationary individuals view compelling visual representations of self motion. It may also occur when detectable lags are present between head movements and recomputations and presentation of the visual display in HMD. Motion sickness is characterized by a diverse set of symptoms but is primarily exemplified by nausea and vomiting. In the case of VEBIM, with adults and adolescents as possible subjects, both including people with psychological and physical problems, the need to verify the problems associated with operating in a virtual environment has to be addressed. The present preliminary study was designed to test VEBIM effects on a non-clinical sample. More in particular the study was designed to: (1) verify the effects provoked by VEBIM on blood pressure and heart rate; (2) verify the effects provoked by VEBIM on the body experience.

Subjects

Sixty subjects (38 males and 22 females: mean age: 23.18 +/-7.54; mean weight: 67.97 Kg +/- 16.23; mean height 173.4 cm +/- 8.16) attending a conference on virtual reality participated in the study.

Procedures

All the subjects were submitted to VEBIM for no more than ten minutes and no less than eight. All the subjects included in the study reached zone 5. No subject experienced zone 6.

Measures

Before the virtual experience the subjects were fitted with a blood pressure cuff and were asked to sit quietly during a 5-minute baseline period. During this period blood pressure and heart rate were recorded. After the virtual experience and after a 10-minute post-task period blood pressure and heart rate were recorded again. Just before entering the virtual environment and just after, all the subjects were submitted to two scales for assessing body experience: the Figure Rating Scale - FRS (Thompson and Altabe, 1991), a set of nine male and female figures which vary in size from underweight to overweight; and the Contour Drawing Rating Scale - CDRS (Thompson and Gray, 1995), a set of nine male and female figures with precisely graduated increments between sizes. In these tests subjects are asked to rate the figures based on the following instructional protocol: (a) current size and (b) ideal size. The difference between the ratings is called "discrepancy index" and is considered to represent the individual's level of dissatisfaction. Both scales have good test-retest reliability.

Statistical Analysis

A power calculation was made to verify the opportunity to obtain statistically significant differences between the pre- and post-virtual reality scores. Given the low statistical power we decided to use exact methods, a series of statistical algorithms developed by the Harvard School of Public Health, that enable researchers to make reliable inferences when data are small, sparse, heavily tied or unbalanced. The exact method used to compare the scores was the marginal homogeneity test (Agresti, 1990).

RESULTS

Concerning the pressure and heart rate scores, no significant difference was found before and after the virtual reality experience. Only one of the subjects experienced simulation sickness. Concerning the body image ratings we found a significant reduction in the FRS and CDRS discrepancy index. This means that after the virtual reality experience the subjects increased their body satisfaction. In both cases the reduction was caused by a decrease in the "ideal body" scores.

CONCLUSIONS

The present study shows that even a short-term application of VEBIM is able to partially reduce the level of body dissatisfaction without any major side effect. The fact that the subjects of our sample view their body as nearer than before the procedure to their ideal means that the virtual environment has induced a more realistic view of their body. As such, the procedure might be helpful in clinical subjects to break through the "resistance" to treatment (Vandereycken, 1990; Vandereycken et al, 1988). Nevertheless, an alteration of the body image toward a more realistic "proportion"—that is, closing the gap between the actual and ideal body image—might be decisive for the long-term outcome. We assume that the virtual experience might be useful to achieve these goal, not as a magic trick but as a catalyzer in a therapeutic process. Of course we have to test both the effects of the virtual environment on a clinical sample and how long the impact of the virtual environment will last. In this preliminary study we have limited the test to just one session, but from a therapeutic viewpoint it seems more reasonable to repeat the procedure.

ACKNOWLEDGMENT

The present work was supported by the Commission of the European Communities (CEC), in particular by the TELEMATICS programme (HC 1053 -Project VREPAR- Virtual Reality Environments for Psycho-neuro-psychological Assessment and Rehabilitation). The author would also like to acknowledge the following people who have contributed to the work described in this paper: Roberto Troiani, Marco Crespi and Gabriele Lissoni from Virtual Sys, Milan; Alessandra Morosin, Paola Regazzoni, Eugenia Borgomainerio, Mirco Bolzoni, Luca Melis and Enrico Molinari from the Centro Auxologico Italiano, Piancavallo; and Carlo Galimberti from the Catholic University of Milan.

A Virtual Reality Application with Autistic Children

Dorothy Strickland, Ph.D.
North Carolina State University

ABSTRACT

Using the advantages of the sense of presence generated by virtual reality, a system to help children with autism was developed. Two case studies with children showed virtual reality has the potential to provide a safer, customized learning environment for individuals with autism. A model of reality which discusses historical and perceptual rules as well as input stimuli in forming a sense of presence is described.

INTRODUCTION

The Americans with Disabilities Act (ADA), Individuals with Disabilities Education Act (IDEA), and Section 504 of the Rehabilitation Act of 1973 have made the education of all children in the United States, including those with special problems, a guaranteed right. Unfortunately, effective treatment methods for children with serious learning problems do not always exist. Individuals with autism have proven particularly difficult to educate. Over half never learn to speak and simple action can take years of personalized instruction. Autism symptomatology involves an internal distortion of the external world. Virtual reality allows controlled distortion of the environment to better match the expectations of an individual. The purpose of this study was to determine if children with autism could respond to virtual reality, and if they might benefit from the controlled, limited-input version of reality that virtual reality can deliver.

AUTISM

High-functioning adult patients who can speak describe an over-powering world, "My hearing is like a hearing aid stuck on 'super loud,'" according to T. Grandin (199).

""I have an interfacing problem, not a core processing problem," writes J. Sinclair. "I can't always keep track of what's happening outside of myself, but I'm never out of touch with my core. Even at worst, when I can't focus and I can't find my body and I can't connect to space and time... I taught myself how to read at 3, and I had to learn again at 10, and yet again at 17, and at 21, and 26. The words that took me 12 years to find have been lost again, and regained, and lost, and still have not come all the way back to where I can be reasonably confident they'll be there when I need them. It wasn't enough to figure out just once how to keep track of my eyes and ears and hands and feet all at the same time; I've lost track of them and had to find them again and again. But I have found them again. The terror is never complete..." Sinclair, 1992).

Definition of Autism

Although there are inconsistent profiles across individuals diagnosed with autism (Tsai, 1992; Ritvo and Freeman, 1978; Rutter, 1978), three commonly found traits involve abnormal response to input stimuli, lack of human engagement, and the inability to generalize between environments. It is postulated that those with autism lack the ability to synthesize input stimuli (Mesibov et al, 1994; Wing, 1972; Des Lauriers, 1969). This profound abnormality in the neurological mechanism controls the capacity to shift attention between different stimuli, leading to distorted sensory input and over selectivity in attention to input stimuli (Courchesne, 1989; Orintz, 1985; Lovaas et al, 1971).

An inability to recognize and process similarities between different scenes may also account for the lack of generalization skills. This results in rigid, limited patterns of action and compulsive or ritualistic behaviors (Rutter, 1968).

Why Virtual Reality May Be Useful With Autism

Both the strengths and limitations of virtual reality appear well matched to the needs of autistic learning tools (Strickland et al, 1995). Features useful in mastering an autistic world and which are attainable with virtual reality include:

Controllable Input Stimuli

Virtual environments can be simplified to the level of input stimuli tolerable by individuals with autism.Distortions in size and character of the components of reality can allow matches to the user's expectations or abilities.Distracting visual complexity, sounds and touch can be removed and introduced in a slow, regulated manner.

Modification for Generalization

Minimal modification across similar scenes may allow generalization and decreased rigidity. A person taught to cross a virtual street in one scene might generalize to another street scene if the differences are reduced until the similarities are recognizable. An example might be two streets which are identical except for one building color.Differences could be increased slowly to teach cross recognition.

Safer Learning Situation

A virtual learning world provides a less hazardous and more forgiving environment for developing skills associated with activities of daily living. Mistakes are less catastrophic and overall stimuli can be reduced. Dynamically adjustable programs permit complex skills, such as judging approaching car speeds when crossing streets, to be tested safely. Environments can be made progressively more complex until realistic scenes help individuals function safely in the real world.

A Primarily Visual World

Virtual reality presently stresses visual responses. Visualization has been effective in teaching abstract concepts to autistic children (Park and Youderian, 1974) and individuals with autism indicate their though patterns are primarily visual (Grandin and Acariano, 1986).

Individualized Treatment

Individuals with autism vary widely in their strengths and weaknesses. Each individual may even demonstrate tremendous variation in skills and behavior between different days (Gregory, 1991; Kaplan and Sadlock, 1990). Given this non-homogeneity of abilities, an individualized approach to placement and training based on a careful, personalized assessment is essential (Schopler, 1987). Computers allow dynamic environments to compensate for changing patterns of development and inconsistent responses.

Learning with Minimal Human Interaction

The complexity of social interaction can interfere when teaching individuals with autism. As early as 1968, computers were used to assist language development therapy with autistic children (Colby, 1968). Advantages of computer learning aids have been reported in multiple studies (Chen and Bernard-Optic, 1993; Plienis and Romanczyk, 1985; Panyan, 1984).

Vestibular Stimulation

An interesting match may exist between latency problems of trackers and abnormal vestibular functioning related to autism. Vestibular confusion appears to be less disturbing to individuals with autism, and in fact may be a positive reinforcer (Grandin, 1992). Sensory integration training intervention have been based, in part, on these vestibular responses (Ray et al, 1988).

A LEARNING TOOL FOR AUTISM

Because of profound variations among people with autism and in-consistencies of response by any one individual from day to day, a case study approach using personalized world modification and assessment was selected for the tests. Two autistic children, a seven-year-old girl and a nine- year-old boy, took part in the study which consisted of over 40 virtual exposures during a six-week period. This allowed reverifica-tion of actions over a series of trials with each child. For safety considerations, no exposure was over five minutes. Both children had been unequivocally diagnosed as autistic, based on test results, parent and therapist reports, behavioral observations and early history. Neither child was classified as high-functioning.

Project Team

The project was a collaborative effort between the North Carolina State University Computer Science and Computer Engineering Departments along with staff and therapists from the Division for Treatment and Education of Autistic and other Communications Handicapped Children (TEACHC) at the University of North Carolina at Chapel Hill School of Medicine. Also active in the tests were parents, siblings, and teachers of the children.

Equipment Used

A ProVision 100 fully integrated virtual reality systems provided by DIVISION Inc. of Chapel Hill, NC was used. The ProVision contained Pixel-Plane hardware for fast image calculation, texture mapping of objects, and true perspective correction at up to 997 million pixels/sec with 24 bit color. Graphics performance was 300 K polygons per second with Phong shading and z-buffering. Software consisted of an object-oriented virtual reality development environment called dVS and a world authoring and simulation program dVISE designed to create virtual worlds on the DIVISION Inc. system. The tracker was a

Polhemus FASTRAK. The headset was the Divisor made by DIVISION Inc. With a field of view of 41 degrees vertically and 105 degrees horizontally, with 75 degrees per eye. Resolution was 345 horizontally by 259 vertical pixels. Stereo images were individually adjusted for the child's smaller IPD.

Learning Situation

The test design chosen was to duplicate a real-life training effort. The initial test was to train a child with autism to recognize a common object, which in our trials was a car within a street scene. Eventually the tests extended to attempting to train a subject to find an object in the environment, walk to it, and stop. Instructional training by therapists, several months previous to our tests, attempted teaching this skill to one of the subjects, with limited success. Eventually, such as skill could lead to the ability to cross a street alone.

Both children were minimally verbal. They could use a few select words such as car and blue, but could neither speak nor understand many normal sentence structures. Their color recognition was limited. To avoid complex instructions or hand controls, a potential problem in the only previous published work which attempted to use a virtual environment with autistic individuals (Kijima et al, 1994), short verbal instructions were used. Responses from the children were either one previously known word or performing the requested actions, such as turning their heads to find a car.

Specialized Test Adaptations

Because of extreme resistance to unfamiliar experiences shown by children with autism, familiar schedules, work, and play activities were introduced into the physical test area. Accustomed patterns from school were duplicated, with the introduction of short, original activities in the virtual helmet spaced between these known activities. A typical test sequence would include a child taking a pre-made schedule consisting of three visual cards clipped to a board, one for 'play' , one for 'work', and one for 'helmet'. One card would have a picture of a play activity.

The child would remove the card from the board, take the picture to a part of the room where there was an envelope with the same picture, deposit the card in the envelop, and then play in that area for several minutes with familiar toys. The child would then be handed the board, he or she would take the next picture from the board and repeat the steps in another part of the room. This technique is part of a structured learning approach emphasized in the TEACHC program and used daily by both children in their normal school environment. When trials deviated from this regimented procedure, the children became agitated and were unwilling to continue the activities.

Many children with autism, including the ones chosen for this study, object to hats or helmets being placed on their heads. The available virtual reality helmet weighed approximately 8 pounds. There was concern that the children would not accept a heavy, enclosed head piece. Attempts were made to acclimate the children to a normal football or riding helmet while at home before the tests began. The girl put on a riding helmet only if she was allowed to go horseback riding. The boy initially refused all helmets but eventually allowed one to be placed on his head.

Older siblings of the children assisted in the tests by wearing the virtual reality helmet and responding appropriately to the virtual environment while the parent attempted to have the autistic child watch, with varying success. The girl always expected to see someone use the helmet first, while the boy would not stay still long enough to watch his sister in the helmet. After the first trial, the sibling was not used again in the boy's tests.

Because the children were unable to verbally express problems or discomfort, helmet wearing was not forced when the child objected. Enticements such as M&Ms (TM) encouraged participation.

Virtual World Design

The virtual world was simplified street scene consisting of a sidewalk and textured building shapes. All motion objects (people, animals, objects in sky) were removed. Periodically one car, whose speed could be set, would pass the child standing on a sidewalk. This test was designed to match the needs of an autistic individual with features of virtual reality in the following ways:

Controllable Input Stimuli

The contrast was kept low in the scenes with gray being the dominant color. The low quality of the headset screens provided a less detailed environment automatically. The cars, the focal point of the test, were presented in bright, contrasting colors. Only car colors recognizable by the individual child we used, in one case this meant colors were limited to red and blue. This distortion allowed us to match the user's input processing abilities while keeping the association of building and car form and functionality.

Modification for Generalization

The patient was place in different positions of the virtual environment at the beginning of different tests. Although all were from the same virtual town, the location on the street varied between trials.

Safer Learning Situation

Freedom to move in a street scene alone without danger was a first for the subjects who normally require constant monitoring in daily activities.

Primarily Visual World

All computer generated stimuli but vision were removed from the virtual world. Padded inserts were placed in front of the helmet speakers within the headset to muffle any hardware feedback sounds. There were verbal instructions to the children.

Individualized Treatment

The worlds were continually modified for each individual to take into account the dynamic response pattern between sessions.

Minimal Human Interaction

Although instructions to the patients were verbal, there were no human images in the virtual world, nor could the subjects see the people in the real world while in the virtual environment.

Vestibular Stimulation

There was no attempt to use virtual induced vestibular stimulation in the tests. Because the training was designed to eventually aid in learning the critical skill of street crossing, environmental responses were kept realistic.

RESULTS

Initially there were serious questions concerning whether children with autism would accept wearing a helmet. If they did, would they recognize an artificial environment when recognizing the real one was so tentative? The results indicated an encouraging adaptation to the technology. One child immediately accepted the virtual helmet and immersed herself to the point that she identified cars and colors. The second child was more rigid and required three sessions, all within a fifteen minute period, to accept the helmet and respond to the scene. Once the helmet was physically accepted, both children would track the cars visually by turning their heads and identifying the cars and their colors. The results of these trials indicated:

Helmet Acceptance

These two autistic children we filmed consistently over the weeks being willing to accept the helmet and guide it onto their heads. Although neither child was adept at verbally expressing sensations, the weight of the helmet became noticeable in the later trials when the children started supporting the front of the helmet with their hands. A lighter helmet is suggested for future trials.

Immersion

The children repeatedly immersed themselves in the virtual scenes to a degree that they verbally labeled objects, colors of objects and tracked virtual moving cars.

Motion in the Virtual World

Once each child repeatedly tracked cars while sitting in a swivel chair, the chair was removed. Both children would wear the helmet while standing and move their bodies within the virtual scenes. All chairs had to be physically removed from the office space in order to get the girl to stand because she preferred spinning in the chair with the helmet on.

A *STOP* sign was attached to the hand controls and moved to different parts of the tracking area during the later tests. The children were asked to find the sign within the scene. This would appear in the virtual world as if the sign moved to different areas of the sidewalk. At times it was difficult to judge the sign's distance because of the lack of comparison cues. This may have contributed to difficulty in the final test sequence which involved stopping at the sign. The children's motions was maintained within the physical range of the Polhemus tracker.

Generalization

The children responded similarly to three different street scenes, but more study needs to be done to determine if they were generalizing across different surroundings.

Learning

Both children were able to turn and find an object in the virtual setting and to walk toward it. One child stopped when reaching the object, which was the new learning exercise. Repeated studies would better verify the response was truly a new learned skill and determine if the skill translated to real world situations. Comparisons of learning times in the virtual versus real world would help verify the value of such a learning technique.

DISCUSSION

The difference between these two children's abilities to find and walk toward a virtual sign appeared related to their understanding of the virtual reality image as an interactive three dimensional world. While neither child could communicate well enough to describe his or her thoughts, actions indicated different responses to the virtual illusion. The virtual scene was simultaneously displayed on a flat screen and in the helmet in order to observe the child's visual world. Although they could not see the screen while in the helmet, both children initially demanded that the flat screen be present before they would accept the helmet.

The two subjects responded differently to the virtual image and the flat screen may provide a clue as to why. The girl freely walked within the illusion, while the boy, when told to "go to sign", would point to the sign inside the helmet. The boy studied the front of the helmet in the initial trials, peering into the plastic as if trying to find the image. He appeared to respond to the world as though it were a scene on a conventional non-virtual-reality computer, while the girl appeared to understand that motions were translatable between the virtual world and real worlds.

The girl also at times pointed to the image in the helmet, but quickly adjusted to walking as a way of getting closer to the sign within the virtual image. In one trial, she stepped over a cord on the floor, indicating that although she understood she could move within the virtual world, she was still aware of the real environment. It was necessary to remove the flat screen in the study with the boy to entice him to stay in the helmet any length of time. The boy had previous extensive experiences with traditional PCS, which may have made it more difficult to adapt to the immersion concept.

CONCLUSIONS

Virtual reality worlds were designed to create a sense of presence in a customized learning scene for two children with autism. A model of reality was used which limited input stimuli. The artificial worlds contained scenes and objects historically identifiable by each child and relied on simple non-conflicting perceptual rules.

These worlds appeared to be accepted and responded to by the two children who took part in this study. The power of the sense of presence in virtual environments seemed encouraging when applied to this new application using virtual reality. Neither child had the verbal ability to understand a description of presence as an abstract term or how the illusion was created with equipment. Their acceptance of objects and actions in the artificial environment was a possible verification of the sense of the presence within the virtual reality.

Although more tests would be necessary to determine the degree of presence the children experienced in the virtual environments, both accepted the new technology and responded with learning actions while in the virtual setting. The acceptance of the immersive qualities of a safe virtual learning situation provides a potentially new tool for furthering efforts at treatment and intervention for autism.

ACKNOWLEDGMENTS

Thanks to the research team of Lee Marcus, Gary Mesibov, and Kerry Hogan from TEACHC; David McAllister from NC State; DIVISION Inc. for loan of the equipment and offices for the test; and to Ed and Jim Bedford, Thea, Larry, and Lauren Gardner, Chris Pratico, Robert Strain, Kayren McNight, Kay Flinn, Donald Merchon, and Libby Webb for their help and ideas.

CHAPTER 8

❖   ❖   ❖

Complementary Research Activities

Immersion, or sense of presence, appears to be the most pronounced factor in VRT. Research has shown, however, that immersion—the feeling of "being there"—is experienced differently by different individuals. Thus, this chapter begins with an innovative research project conducted by Dr. Joseph Psotka and Dr. Sharon Davison, who studied the cognitive factors associated with immersion. Their findings are partially reported here. This unique preliminary research provides us with a useful instrument for screening potential subjects for VRT. The second section briefly describes an experiment that investigated the relationship between sense of presence in the virtual environment and sense of presence in the physical world. This research project was designed by Dr. Max North and conducted by Mr. Rodney Swift and Miss Adrienne Raglin at the U.S. Army Center of Excellence in Research on Training.

Another important finding is that learning occurs while patients are under the influence of VRT. The learning appears to be activated by intrinsic motivation which in turn lengthens the time that VRT can hold the patient's attention. This issue is discussed in a research project conducted by Professor Sarah North, co-author of this book. Her research explores the effect of virtual reality in the motivation processes of learners. The multimedia version of this research report may be found in the *International Journal of Virtual Reality*, Volume 2, No. 1,

1996. An extended abstract can be found in the *Electronic Journal of Virtual Culture*, winter issue, 1996.

These reports give us insight into the nature of immersion and its effects, introducing some assertions as to why and how VRT works. It must be noted that these research findings are preliminary. Researchers currently are testing their initial hypotheses with larger groups of subjects.

Cognitive Factors Associated with Immersion in Virtual Environments

Joseph Psotka, Ph.D. and Sharon Davison, Ph.D.
U. S. Army Research Institute and Catholic University

Immersion into the dataspace provided by a computer, and the feeling of really being there or "presence," are commonly acknowledged as the uniquely important features of virtual reality environments. How immersed one feels appears to be determined by a complex set of physical components and affordances of the environment, as well as psychological processes that as yet are poorly understood. Pimentel and Teixeira (1993) say that the experience of being immersed in a computer-generated world involves the same mental shift of "suspending your disbelief for a period of time" as "when you get wrapped up in a good novel or become absorbed in playing a computer game." While this sounds logical, evidence for these conclusions is required. The basic precondition for understanding Virtual Reality is understanding the spatial representation systems that localize our bodies or egocenters in space (Franklin et al, 1992).The effort to understand these cognitive processes is being driven with new energy by the pragmatic demands of successful virtual reality environments, but the literature is largely sparse and anecdotal (Benedikt, 1991; Ellis et al, 1991; Furness, 1993; Laurel, 1991; Pimentel and Teixeira, 1993; Witmer and Singer, in preparation). Although virtual reality literature pays a great deal of lip service to the perceptual psychology of J. J. Gibson, there is little in the ecological perception framework that might suggest sources of individual differences in the quality of immersion. Yet, anecdotally, there appear to be wide differences in how well people react to these exotic environments.

In a first step to gather more information, a focused set of questions was compiled into two questionnaires: a measure of susceptibility and a measure of the depth of visual immersion. These were sent to users of virtual reality environments over the Internet on the virtu-l listserv.

The questions were carefully designed to cover cognitive factors that have been discussed in the literature on virtual reality environments. By and large, the literature has not raised a very detailed or analytic set of questions, so many questions we developed deal with issues that have face value only. For instance, Pimentel and Teixeira (1993; p. 105) offer the following set of factors as instrumental for deep immersion: interactivity, fast update rate, high image complexity, engaging, 3D sound, head-mounted display; stereoscopic; large field of view, and head tracking. None of these are cognitive factors, although they admit that a "holistic technique might be necessary because the experience of immersion is more than just the mere sum of its parts."

DESIGN

Stimuli

The factors we considered for this preliminary study were grouped into two categories: A. Susceptibility to immersion; and B. Quality of immersion.

A. Susceptibility to immersion:
  I. Imagination
        Strength of visual imagination
        Dreaming
        Self-consciousness
        Daydreaming
        Ability to willingly suspend disbelief
        Depth of involvement in books, theater, etc.
  II. Vivid Imagery
        Dreaming
        Prior expectations about the virtual reality environments

Claustrophobia
III. Concentration and Attention
Attentional filtering
Cognitive conflict in holding two recursive immersions
Spatial Navigation
Claustrophobia
IV. Self-control
Self-control
Active participation and catharsis

B. Quality of immersion:
  I. Affordances of the Virtual Reality Environment for Immersion:
    Object Persistence
    Sensory Completeness
    Interactivity
    Realism of the environment
    Amount of lag or delay
    Size of field of view
    Accuracy of egocenter or body image location
    Pleasure and exhilaration from the novelty of the experience
  II. Distractions from the Real Environment:
    Presence of others; sounds, tactile
    Fatigue and irritation by bulky equipment
    Restrictiveness of the equipment
    Similarity of Real World to Virtual Reality World
  III. Physiological effects
    Simulator sickness
    Disorientation after immersion
  IV. Other Effects
    Prefer immersion alone
    Surprise when Head-Mounted Display removed

Many other factors could be assessed, but for the first effort it was important to keep the questionnaire short to elicit as many voluntary responses as possible, and to begin winnowing these factors in a sensible way.

The constructed questionnaire used 12 questions for the susceptibility component (that might also be used as a pre-test in any experimental setting) and 11 questions to measure the quality of immersion. All questions were constructed on a five-point categorical (Likert) scale for responses. The questionnaire is shown in the following section, with some changes and new questions that have been added through the preliminary analysis reported here. The questions were asked so that roughly half of them were constructed to relate positively with depth of immersion and half negatively. A key was constructed to convert all questions to positive relationships. For convenience, we have included the questionnaires here.

QUESTIONNAIRE

Please answer these questions. They are intended to provide us some insight into the process of "immersion" and the nature of "presence". You will be asked another questionnaire after you "walk" through the model of a house we have designed with our special "head-mounted display".

PRE-TEST: A questionnaire to try to measure someone's susceptibility to experiencing a pleasurable immersion into virtual reality.

1. *Do you dream in color?*
    [Never], [Seldom], [Sometimes], [Often], [Always]

2. *How realistic do you think this experience will be visually?*
    [Photo Real], [Like Movies], [Like TV], [Like Comics], [Blurred]

3. *Do you feel claustrophobic or uneasy in small spaces?*
    [Never], [Seldom], [Sometimes], [Often], [Always]

4. *When you speak in public, how self-conscious do you feel?*
    [Totally], [Very], [Somewhat], [A Little], [Not At All]

5. *How often have you cried watching a good, sad movie?*
    [Never], [Seldom], [Sometimes], [Often], [Always]

6. *How engrossing is a good book?*
    [Totally], [Very], [Somewhat], [A Little], [Not At All]

7. *How often have you stayed up late to finish a good book?*
    [Never], [Seldom], [Sometimes], [Often], [Always]

8. *How often do you daydream?*
    [Never], [Seldom], [Sometimes], [Often], [Always]

9. Can you read in a moving car, boat, or plane?
    [Never], [Seldom], [Sometimes], [Often], [Always]

10. Do you keep track of where you are when some one else is driving?
    [Never], [Seldom], [Sometimes], [Often], [Always]

11. How important is it to be completely in control?
    [Totally], [Very], [Somewhat], [A Little], [Not At All]

12. How often have people told you they called your name and you have no recollection
    of hearing them while watching TV, or reading a book?
    [Never], [Seldom], [Sometimes], [Often], [Always]

13. How realistic and detailed are your usual visual images, such as of your car or of
    a good friend?
    [Totally], [Very], [Somewhat], [A Little], [Not At All]

14. How much do you prefer improvisation and exploration over
    following directions?
    [Totally], [Very], [Somewhat], [A Little], [Not At All]

15. How often as a child did you play pretend or make - believe?
    [Never], [Seldom], [Sometimes], [Often], [Always]

POST-TEST: *A questionnaire to try to measure the depth of someone's immersion into
    virtual reality.*

1. When you removed the Head mounted display, how surprised were you at the
    direction you were facing?
    [Totally], [Very], [Somewhat], [A Little], [Not At All]

2. During the immersion how aware were you of the direction you faced in the real
    world?
    [Totally], [Very], [Somewhat], [A Little], [Not At All]

3. How often did you think of the other person(s) in the real world with you?
    [Never], [Seldom], [Sometimes], [Often], [Always]

4. How much more enjoyable would it have been to have the immersion experience
    with no one else in the room?
    [Totally], [Very], [Somewhat], [A Little], [Not At All]

6. How completely did you believe you were part of the virtual environment?
    [Totally], [Very], [Somewhat], [A Little], [Not At All]

7. When you turned your back on an object in the virtual environment, was it still there?
    [Never], [Seldom], [Sometimes], [Often], [Always]

8. How flat and missing in depth did the virtual reality world appear?
    [Totally], [Very], [Somewhat], [A Little], [Not At All]

9. How woozy or nauseous did you feel after the experience?
    [Totally], [Very], [Somewhat], [A Little], [Not At All]

10. How exhilarated did you feel after the experience?
    [Totally], [Very], [Somewhat], [A Little], [Not At All]

11. How disoriented did you feel after the experience?
    [Totally], [Very], [Somewhat], [A Little], [Not At All]

Additional Questions:

12. How disturbing was the lag or delay between your movements in the real world and the virtual reality world?
    [Totally], [Very], [Somewhat], [A Little], [Not At All]

13. How often did you feel your body image was in the wrong place in the virtual reality world?
    [Never], [Seldom], [Sometimes], [Often], [Always]

15. How natural and realistic was any object motion?
    [Totally], [Very], [Somewhat], [A Little], [Not At All]

16. How much narrower was the field of view than normally?
    [Totally], [Very], [Somewhat], [A Little], [Not At All]

17. How completely could you search the environment visually?
    [Totally], [Very], [Somewhat], [A Little], [Not At All]

18. How realistic was this experience visually?
    [Photo Real], [Like Movies], [Like TV], [Like Comics], [Blurred]

19. How completely did you adapt to the virtual reality world and its special characteristics?
    [Totally], [Very], [Somewhat], [A Little], [Not At All]

20. How completely were all your senses engaged by the virtual reality world?
    [Totally], [Very], [Somewhat], [A Little], [Not At All]

21. How often did images of the virtual reality world intrude in your daily life or your dreams after the experience?
[Never], [Seldom], [Sometimes], [Often], [Always]

Subjects

Fifteen respondents whose gender is unknown had some experience in a variety of virtual reality environments ranging from homebred PC systems to state of the art centers at University North Carolina, BBN, Chicago, and the Human Interface Technology Laboratory at University of Washington. The modal virtual reality environment was the W. Industries' Virtuality Arcade with seven respondents. Most of the respondents had less than one hour of experience in virtual reality environments. Eight responses came from individuals with no virtual reality environment experience, who only answered the questionnaire dealing with susceptibility.

These are very small numbers of respondents for the factor analyses used in this exploratory study. The results must be viewed as provisional, reflecting some of our biases as well as true relationships between cognitive components and depth of immersion. Ideally, 100 respondents for each group would be welcome. This would even begin to allow comparisons among the different virtual reality environments used by the respondents.

RESULTS

Pre-test

On the susceptibility to immersion questionnaire, no significant differences were found in the scores of the group with no virtual reality experience and the group with some virtual reality experience, using a standard analysis of variance ($f=0.45$, $df=13$, $p=0.51$). The two groups' scores correlated significantly ($r=0.63$, $df=13$, $p<0.05$). On the whole, they often dream in color; think that the quality of virtual reality is like TV; occasionally feel claustrophobic or uneasy in small spaces; feel somewhat self conscious speaking in public; have sometimes cried watching a good, sad movie; find a good book very engrossing; have sometimes stayed up late to finish a good book; daydream often; are often able to read in a moving car, boat, or plane; can often tell where they are when some one else is driving; feel it is somewhat important to be completely in control; and have occasionally been told that their name was called when watching TV or reading a book, but have not recollection of hearing it.

Post-test

On the actual experience of virtual environments, the critical question that asked how completely people believed they were part of the virtual environment yielded only a modest "somewhat." However, on the whole, they felt "very" exhilarated by the experience. More than half the respondents reported they were "very" or "totally" exhilarated. The difference may be that more than half of them felt a little or more woozy or nauseous from the experience. Given their short stays in these virtual environments, that may be a reason for concern.

Most of them felt somewhat surprised by the direction they were facing when they removed the head-mounted display. On the whole, this left no aftereffect, and they reported that they were only a little disoriented by the experience. They continued on the whole to be somewhat aware of the direction they faced in the real world during the virtual reality experience. They occasionally or sometimes thought about the other person(s) in the real world with them there. Most of them felt that other person(s) made no difference to their enjoyment of the experience.

Almost all of the respondents complained that the virtual reality devices restricted their movements somewhat or a lot. The bulkiness of current equipment should make that a surprise to no one.

Most of them reported that when they turned their back on an object in the virtual reality environment, it was still there (although some commented that they might not easily find it again). This is a cognitive skill called "object permanence" or "existence constancy" by psychologists. It is part of a Piagetian test of maturation for children, and may be a good index of the maturity of virtual reality environments too.

There was considerable variability in how flat and missing in depth the virtual reality world appeared, as might be expected from the range of equipment, but on the whole it was only a little missing in depth.

Correlations

Many significant correlations were found ($r = 0.47$, df=13, p=0.05). Two sets of correlations might be interpreted. One set looks at the questions within each of the two questionnaires for common factors of importance. The other looks at the correlations between the two questionnaires to try to guess at causal or dynamic connections among susceptibility and the quality of immersion. Principal components factor analysis was used with oblique varimax transformations to select the factors reported below.

Causal or dynamic connections between susceptibility and the quality of immersion: The results were examined for each question that asked about the quality of the experience for a correlation that significantly affected it. These correlations are reported in terms of rules below.

Overview

Immersion was most affected by how claustrophobic one is. The more claustrophobic you are the more often you think about the other person(s) in the real world with you there. The more you complained that virtual reality devices restricted your movements, the less often you felt objects were still there when you turned your back on them. The less exhilarated by the experience you were, the more nauseous or woozy you felt. Clearly this is a danger signal for arcade makers of virtual reality environments. Rather than providing access to a wide open cyberspace, current equipment is still evoking claustrophobic feelings of enclosure and restriction. While almost half of the respondents reported no wooziness or nausea after the experience, this is a pretty extreme response, and arcade makers should flag the fact that more than half reported a "little" or "some" wooziness or nausea. Apparently, those who are somewhat susceptible to claustrophobia, and in this small sample 9 of the 15 reported some sensitivity, have this fear triggered by current equipment.

Depth of immersion was most strongly predicted by whether or not you dream in color, by how often you cry at good, sad movies, and by how effectively you filter out other distractions while reading a book or watching TV. You are more deeply immersed if you dream often in color and you ignore others when they call you while reading or watching TV. You also are more deeply immersed if you are more exhilarated by the experience. There appear to be two psychological factors dominant in predicting depth of immersion. One is the willingness to accept another reality and the willingness to make the effort it takes to participate in it fully and satisfactorily. This factor is dominated by crying at movies, staying up late, and being engrossed by a book. It suggests that childhood pretend play and make believe were a significant part of a person's experience. The other factor depends on the ability to shut out the distracting effects of the real world. This factor is implicated in ignoring others when they call you while you are watching TV, and being able to shut out the real world when you wake up dreaming. This factor may be seriously tested as more complex virtual reality systems become available, that integrate virtual worlds with reality into a new augmented reality.

Exhilaration and enjoyment of the experience are also increased if you are not claustrophobic, and you do not think self control is very important. Two individuals were strongly claustrophobic, and their exhilaration scores were markedly lower than the others'. Exhilaration was also increased if you believed you were deeply immersed and that objects behind your back continued to exist.

Summary of Susceptibility for Immersion

Relationships among the questions are given as rules in the following section. Several clusters are revealed by these intercorrelations.

Summary of Susceptibility for Immersion Responses:

Question 1. If you tend to dream in color you believe the virtual reality world will be more photorealistic, and you seldom feel claustrophobic.

Question 2. If you expect the virtual reality world to be more cartoon - like and blurred you tend not to dream in color, and you tend not to be able to read in a moving car.

Question 3. If you tend to be claustrophobic you rarely dream in color.

Question 4. If you are self-conscious you find a good book engrossing and you seldom daydream.

Question 5. If you often cry at a good, sad movie you stay up late to finish a good book, you can read in a moving car, and you find it important to be in control.

Question 6. If you tend to find a good book engrossing you tend to stay up late to finish a good book, you cry more often at good, sad movies, and you find it important to be in control.

Question 7. If you tend to stay up late to finish a good book you tend to find a good book engrossing, you cry more often at good, sad movies, and you find it important to be in control.

Question 8. If you tend to daydream more often you are not self conscious and you find a good book engrossing.

Question 9. If you tend to be able to read in a moving car you tend to dream in color, you believe the virtual reality world will be more photorealistic, and you seldom feel claustrophobic

Question 10. No significant correlations.

Question 11. The more important you feel it is to be completely in control. the more you tend to cry at good, sad movies, the more engrossing a good book is, and the more often you stay up late to finish a good book.

Cluster A (35% of the Variance) Imagination: Questions 4, 6, 7 and 8 intercorrelated. These all deal with self-consciousness, daydreaming, and how engrossing a book is, even staying up late to finish reading it. Attentional control and ignoring distractions may be the dominant factors. Especially in arcades, wearing the gear required for virtual reality experiences may make some people feel foolish and disturb their immersion. Being willing and able to use your imagination seems to be a common thread.

Cluster B (29 % of Variance) Vividness of Imagery and Claustro-phobia: Questions 1, 2, 3, and 9 intercorrelated. 1 and 2 deal with how often you dream in color and how realistic you think the virtual reality world will be visually, while 3 and 9 relate to motion sickness and claustrophobia. The link between those two is unknown. Perhaps there is an unknown relationship between being able to remember dreams in sufficient detail to remember color, (since we all dream every night, probably in color) and our ability to deal with motion sickness and claustrophobia. Our favorite explanation, derived from discussions with our colleague Peter Legree, postulates that the common thread is an ability to shut out or exclude the unwanted effects of the environment. Obviously this is important for claustrophobics when they try to control their claustrophobia in small spaces.

Shutting out reality is also important for those who want to remember their dreams. Most dream memories are only accessible in the first few moments of waking, a special twilight period when both realities are accessible to people. If you can shut out the world during this brief period, you will remember your dreams more clearly, including the fact that they are in color. Most of us who have tried to recall our dreams over an extended period have found that our ability to hold on to this twilight period when dreams are accessible increases with practice, but some of us continue to find it easier than others. It appears that parts of this ability are a skill that can be learned, but other parts may be controlled by psychological processes that are more difficult to change. It appears that they may also affect the depth of immersion in today's crude virtual reality environments.

Why this factor contains expectations of the photorealism of the virtual reality world is also not immediately explicable. Again, our favorite story is that the expected realism of the virtual reality world depends on the vibrancy of dream worlds compared to the real world. Those who can remember their dreams in vivacious detail may be expected to have higher and similar expectations for the virtual reality experience. These expectations also seem to influence the depth of the immersion experience, since those who expect too much appear to be disappointed.

Cluster C (19% of Variance) Self Control: Questions 5 and 11 intercorrelated. These both deal with some components of self control and attentional control. Crying at movies deals with issues of immersion that are under voluntary and imaginative control, rather than the involuntary and ecological or environmental imposition of immersion that we normally experience in our day to day interaction with the environment. Crying at movies also demands the willingness and skill to be able to achieve catharsis (Laurel, 1992) from the fantasy experience of the virtual reality world. Crying at the movies is a pleasurable experience, not an unhappy one. It does not come easily, but demands that viewers participate actively in the movie, and engage its themes and personal events in a powerful way that releases emotions safely, and without fear of personal injury. It demands involvement and participation in an interactive way, and may be related to how satisfying childhood pretend play and make-believe were. Movies and virtual reality experiences are thrilling and emotionally satisfying because they are safe and they are fantasy. If you did not know that it was a fantasy, the events would be horrifying and deeply unsatisfying; yet, because they are fantasy the experience can be deep and meaningful, but quite pleasurable too. Unlike dreaming, where it is important to shut out the distractions of the real world, cathartic release in movies depends on actively engaging and participating in the movie, and actively suspending your disbelief about its illusion. It is interesting that this skill appears to be more positive and affirming than the negative act of shutting out distractions, that appeared in the first factor.

Cluster D (17% of the Variance): Questions 10 and 12 intercorrelated. These both deal with being able to do two things at the same time: pay attention to where you are going when someone else is driving; and listening for others who call you while watching TV. This factor may hinge on the skill of holding two or more realities in mind at the same time. Being able to concentrate and disregard the opinion of others seems to be a common thread.

Summary of Depth of Immersion Responses

The responses and intercorrelations for each question are given in the following section. Several clusters are revealed by these intercorrelations.

Summary of Depth of Immersion Responses:

Question 1. If you are more surprised by the direction you are facing when the HMD is removed, you become disoriented by the experience, and when object constancy is accepted in the virtual environment.

Question 2. If you tend to be more aware of the direction you are facing in the real world, while you are immersed, you think of other people in the real world, you tend to feel that the virtual reality devices are restrictive, and you tend to become woozy or nauseous.

Question 3. If you tend to think about the other person(s) in the real world with you there you tend to be more aware of the direction you are facing in the real world, you tend to feel that the virtual reality devices are restrictive, and the world tends to feel flat and missing in depth.

Question 4. No significant correlations.

Question 5. If you find the virtual reality devices restrictive you tend to be more aware of the direction you are facing in the real world, you tend to think about the other person(s) in the real world with you there, and the world tends to be less flat and missing in depth.

Question 6. If you tend to believe completely that you were a part of the virtual reality world, your object constancy is strong in the virtual reality environment, and the experience tends to be very exhilarating.

Question 7. If your object constancy is strong in the virtual reality environment you are more surprised by the direction you are facing when the HMD is removed, you tend to believe completely that you were a part of the virtual reality world, and the experience tends to be very exhilarating.

Question 8. If the world tends to be less flat and missing in depth you tend to be more aware of the direction you are facing in the real world, while you are immersed, you tend to think about the other person(s) in the real world with you there, and you find the virtual reality devices restrictive.

Question 9. If you become more woozy and nauseous you tend to be more aware of the direction you are facing in the real world, while you are immersed.

Question 10. If the experience tends to be very exhilarating you tend to believe completely that you were a part of the virtual reality world and your object constancy is strong in the virtual reality environment.

Question 11. If you are more disoriented you are more surprised by the direction you are facing when the HMD is removed.

Cluster A (32% of Variance) Distractibility: Questions 2, 3, 5, and 8 intercorrelated. They all deal with potential distractions outside of the virtual reality environment that could diminish the depth of immersion and the feeling of presence. The direction you face in the real world, how often you think of others in the real world, how restricted your movement is, how flat and missing in depth the world appears, all potentially distract you from the immersion experience. The flatness or lack of depth question was intended to pertain to the virtual reality world, but perhaps people took it to apply to the real world after coming out of the virtual reality experience.

Cluster B (26% of Variance) Willingness to Suspend Disbelief: Questions 6, 7 and 10 intercorrelated. These all deal with those components of the automatic or ecological affordances of the environment that control the depth of immersion, and since they include the prime measure of depth of belief in being part of the environment, they must be more central to the whole immersion experience: sense of object permanence, exhilaration in the experience—these are all involuntary effects of deep immersion. This is perhaps why they all correlate with dreaming in color, since that too is an involuntary immersion and acceptance of another reality, the reality of unconscious imagery and dreams. If one can accept the reality of these still crude cartoons and interactive computer displays, then it may not take an act of self control and will power, but a state of mind that is open and susceptible to altered states of consciousness, like dreams. Notice that dreams are not like daydreams, a meandering of conscious ideas, and it is instructive that daydreaming does not correlate with any of these measures of ecological immersion. It is only the basic involuntary and biological but complex act of dreaming, a total immersion in a hallucinogenic other reality that provides the best measure of immersion into virtual reality environments.

Cluster C (24% of Variance) Concentration: Questions 1 and 4 intercorrelated. They ask how much more enjoyable the experience would have been without anyone else around, and how surprised you were when the HMD was removed. Apparently this did not affect the depth of immersion of people who were distracted by the presence of others, nor make them think of others, so it is not related to their distractibility. However, some people must find fantasy in an immersion environment more enjoyable when they are alone, perhaps because they are self-conscious and cannot concentrate on the experience. Surprise on removing the HMD gives a measure of the concentration on the task of immersion.

Cluster D (19% of the Variance) Simulation Sickness Effects: Questions 9 and 11 intercorrelated. These both deal with how disoriented and how woozy or nauseous you feel. These side effects of immersion also have a strong influence on the depth of the immersion experience. Surprisingly, we did not ask about the effects of lag or apparent body position, so dizziness and nausea were only related to being aware of the direction you faced in the real world.

Overall Correlations between Pre-test and Post-test

The correlation between the Susceptibility measure and the Total Immersion scale was (r =0.82, df=13, p<0.01). This significant correlation suggests that our measure of immersion susceptibility offers the minimal requirement for prediction—significant correlation of the intended measure.

DISCUSSION

The most interesting component of these results is that immersion can be seen as a dual phenomenon. On the one hand dependent on implicit or subconscious biological processes and skills that invoke our cognitive machinery only when the affordances of the ecological setting is suitable; and on the other hand dependent on voluntary attentional skills that depend on self control, self-consciousness, distractibility, attention, expectations, and will power. These two factors (implicit versus conscious control of immersion) are captured in one correlation.

Immersion is most complete if you dream in color. How these two components interact is a powerful mystery. The two implicit and conscious components appear to do different things and may not be capable of affecting each other directly. These factors come out so strongly that they are visible in all three sets of correlations: in the susceptibility factors, in the immersion factors, and in their intercorrelations. The fact that they are so strong in the susceptibility factors may indicate that people were interpreting these questions in a very special way, since they had already experienced virtual reality immersion. A larger sample may introduce differences between those who are and are not experienced in virtual reality, on the responses to the susceptibility questionnaire. It must be remembered that these results came from people who answered both questionnaires at the same time, not in the way they were intended to be used—before and after experiencing immersion. However, this standardization group is still important for the kinds of intercorrelations it demonstrates.

Implicit factors have a kind of dominance. It may not be possible to overlook certain ecological preconditions for immersion if they are violated, no matter how intent one may be to have a deep immersive experience. For example, if the lag between intention and visual feedback of perceived hand movement in the virtual reality world is very large, no amount of mental filtering of the image is likely to reduce that lag; and it may lead to varying degrees of simulator sickness. Or, as another example, if your visual system tells you that your egocenter or body image is in one location, but your kinesthetic senses locate it somewhere else, there may be no way to override or integrate these two positions by cognition alone. Longer term processes of learning and adaptation that change the cognitive machinery may be required.

From these results, it appears that immersion in a virtual reality world is not like being immersed in a book or a good movie. It appears to be more like remembering your dreams. Unlike a book or a movie there are strong visual affordances for immersion in your dreams. There you are almost always the agent of action and interaction, and there is only one world in which you are immersed. When you look at a picture or build up a representation of the space described in a book (Franklin, Tversky and Coon, 1992) that fact that you are sitting or standing in another (real) space never quite gets forgotten, so there must always still be some sort of conflict between the two representations of your egocenter.

This conflict is most evident when you look at a picture, either a photograph or a painting. Particularly in paintings, the viewpoint of the painting is often quite controlled and striking (Kubovy, 1986). In Davinci's famous painting of the last supper, for instance, the viewpoint is elevated some 5 meters above the floor of the room where most people stand to view it. Art critics have suggested that this is to give one the feeling of elevation and levitation as one views the painting. Most viewers are unaware of the conflict between their egocenter as people in the room and their apparent egocenter as viewers in the painting. The space of the painting and the space of the room are shared easily. This is unlike virtual reality immersion where entering the virtual reality world depends on blocking out the real world almost completely. This happens in the real world when someone holds a mask in front of their face too. Holding a picture in front of your face has a disturbing effect a mask does not, because the space of the picture and the space of your face are so different that it is not really possible to reconcile them. Surely conflicts between visual and kinesthetic egocenters are being resolved continuously in the real world, since all of our systems are slightly in error in our interactions with the world.

It is very important to proceed with the categorization of the cognitive and perceptual components of immersion, and continue this analysis. Take for instance the primary cognitive process of specifying an egocenter within a cognitive spatial representation system. Clearly the location of the egocenter is computed from many visual cues, derived from the structure of the optic array. In a virtual reality system many differences between an ecologically mimetic representation and the real world could yield either less presence, or inaccurate immersion, or both. For instance, a narrower field of view could destroy the experience of immersion as others have suggested, not in and of itself, but because it also created a displaced egocenter, or created the illusion of viewing the world through a porthole or goggles from outside the world.

Entering the virtual reality world appears to require the full and complete use of psychological spatial representation processes that normally appear to be able to allocate only one spatial egocenter at a time. Franklin, Tversky and Coon, (1992) report that readers will try to encompass only one described scene at a time, and cannot easily integrate two different locations and scenes. Holding on to reality in a virtual reality experience appears to be equally difficult, and so the distractibility of the environment and the equipment used for the virtual reality representation become critical factors in the depth of the virtual reality experience.

Fleshing out the cognitive and perceptual components of immersion promises to be a long but rewarding task. It is particularly rewarding for training and educational purposes because we already know that so much of cognitive representation is in the form of mental models for understanding complex systems. Virtual reality promises to turn knowledge into experience and make education and training much more direct and effective.

ACKNOWLEDGMENTS

The Opinions in this paper do not necessarily imply or express the view of the U.S. Army Research Institute (USARI). This research was funded by the USARI Research and Advanced Applications Office and conducted with many fine colleagues: Sharon A. Davison, Sonya A. Lewis, Mark Pflaging, Sandy Ressler, and Marc Sebrechts. I thank Bob Seidel for many stimulating discussions, and Veronica Pantelidis and Chris Dede for detailed reviews and many fine suggestions.

The Sense of Presence in a Virtual Environment Navigation and Target Detection Experiment

*Max M. North, Ph.D., Rodney Swift, M.S.D., and
Adrienne Raglin, M.S.E.E.*
**U.S. Army Center of Excellence in Research on Training,
Morris Brown College &
Army Research Laboratory, Software Technology Branch**

INTRODUCTION

The sense of presence that users experience in a virtual environment is perhaps the best-known attribute of virtual reality. It is an appeal to this sense of presence that is used to distinguish virtual reality as something different from merely a multimedia system or an interactive computer graphics display.However, our basic understanding of "presence" is still primarily anecdotal in nature. We have yet to rigorously explore basic questions about the nature of presence. The primary objective of this research study was to investigate the relationship between the sense of presence in the virtual environment and the sense of presence of the physical world while immersed in the virtual environment.

METHOD

Sixteen subjects (nine male and seven female) participated in this study. The virtual environment system for this study consisted of a Pentium-based processing unit, a stereoscopic head-mounted display (VR4, Virtual Reality Inc.), an electromagnetic 6D multi-receiver/transmitter head-tracking device (Flock of Birds, Ascension Technology Corp.), a steering device for navigating through virtual environment, and a foot pedal which enabled the participants to stop at the time they detected a specific target within the virtual environment. The VREAM Virtual Reality Development Software Package and Libraries were used to create the virtual environment scene for this study. The questionnaires used for this study was the Sense of Presence Scale in the Virtual Environment and the Physical Environment. These questionnaires were designed to assess one's sense of presence of the virtual environment and the physical environment, sense of interactivity of virtual environment system, and one's perception of the real world in reflection to the virtual environment. Participants were given the questionnaires after completing one set of 60 trials with each trial lasting approximately a minute. There were a total of seven trials given over a two day period. The virtual environment scene for this study was created intentionally very simple with no distracting objects presented in the scene. This arrangement provided us with a very low level of details that allowed us to measure the sense of presence with minimal visual cues available to participants. Subjects were given several conditions and tasks to perform within the virtual environment to load their cognitive processing and pull them into the virtual environment scene. For example, one of the conditions was that the participants must react to signs that appeared on the road at any given time. Specifically, subjects were told to navigate a vehicle on the road and detect a specific possible target of a certain shape and color that might pop in front of them.

PRELIMINARY RESULTS AND CONCLUSIONS

The subjective measures of the sense of presence in the virtual environment increased gradually after each session while the subjective measure of sense of physical environment while attending the virtual environment decreased gradually across sessions. The results led to the conclusion that the longer subjects remained in the virtual environment the higher their sense of presence became, even though scenes were purposely created with a very low level of details. At the same time, the subjects' sense of presence of the real physical environment decreased. This attests to a theory that the sense of presence is constant and that subjects have to give up the sense of presence in one environment to achieve it in the other one.

The Effectiveness of the Virtual Environments in the Motivational Processes of the Learners

Sarah M. North, M.S.D.
Virtual Reality Technology Laboratory
Clark Atlanta University

ABSTRACT

This paper reports on the use of virtual environments and their effectiveness in improving on and maintaining learners' intrinsic motivation or interest. The study employed objects as stimuli in the physical world and virtual world which had to be manipulated and arranged in nine different patterns. The results led to the conclusion that virtual reality technology can stimulate learners' curiosity and interest, and heighten their sense of control.

INTRODUCTION

Virtual Reality (virtual environments) offers a new Human-Computer Interaction paradigm in which users are no longer simply external observers of data or images on a computer screen but are active partic- ipants within a computer-generated three-dimensional virtual world (Fontaine, 1992; Held, and Durlach, 1992; North and North, 1994; North et al, 1995a).

Consistent with Piagetian thinking, research suggests that children's interactive experiences with computers provide opportunities for them to actively explore, test, create, invent new activities and observe the outcome of their efforts (Haugland and Shade, 1988; Schetz, 1994). Researchers postulate that when children have meaningful interactions with discovery-oriented, open-ended software, the computer becomes an important teaching tool.

The primary purpose of this research was to carry out a study of the effectiveness of virtual reality on improving and maintaining learners' intrinsic motivation or interest. By providing virtual environments that stimulate curiosity, interest, and a sense of control, learners can be taught to generate their own motivational strategies. Since the virtual environment provides a sense of presence and intuitive interaction techniques, it may be possible to create scenarios to stimulate the learners' curiosity and interest.

METHOD

Eighteen Clark Atlanta University students, 11 males and seven females, between 21 and 32 years old, served as subjects for the study. The experiment consisted of a physical world environment, in which wooden blocks were used, and a virtual world, in which virtual blocks were used. Both worlds used color and shape as variables. The two variables consisted of three shapes (sphere, pyramid, and cube), and three colors (red, green, and blue). In both worlds, the wooden blocks and virtual blocks had to be manipulated and arranged in nine different patterns. Data gloves were worn to manipulate, interact with and navigate the objects in the virtual world. Each subject was given a demonstration of how to handle the materials used in the two worlds and was tested individually. The first experiment started with a two-block pattern. At each step, the difficulty was increased by increasing the number of blocks. The subject's score was based on a ten-point scale instrument administered at the end of each experiment. The scores ranged from very weak to very strong.

RESULTS

The results were used to identify the significance of difference between the subjects' performance in the virtual world and physical world with respect to curiosity, interest and sense of control. The interest level comparison indicated that for all subjects, scores (N=8, Mean=7.45, S.D.=1.28) in the virtual world were always higher than the scores (N=8, Mean=4.75, S.D.=3.97) in the physical world (N=8, t =1.82, df=14), (Figure 1). The sense of control level comparison indicated that scores (N=8, Mean=10.20, S.D.=4.47) in the virtual world were not always higher than the scores (N=8, Mean=4.04, S.D.=3.44) in the physical world in the beginning (N=8, t =2.89, df=14). However, after orientation to navigation through the virtual environment, the mean score rose gradually (Figure 2).

CONCLUSION

This research demonstrates that the virtual world is more useful than the physical world (with respect to color and shape) in increasing the memory span of the learner. Based on observation, it was apparent that each subject was excited and enthusiastic, and more eager to be in the virtual environment than the physical environment.

The main conclusions of this research are as follows:

- Memory span increases significantly more in the virtual world than in the physical world.
- When subjects have enough interaction "pulled into" the virtual world, memory span increases significantly.
- Compared to the real world, the subjects' cognitive resources increased in virtual reality.
- Virtual reality stimulates learners' motivation, comprehension and interest for a longer period of time.

ACKNOWLEDGMENT

This research project was sponsored by a grant from Boeing Computer Services and the U.S. Army Research Laboratory (Contract Number DAAL03-92-6-0377). Thanks are extended to Latonya Smith, and Sharon Hicks, Jamie Hamilton, and Derick Nelson for participating in this research.

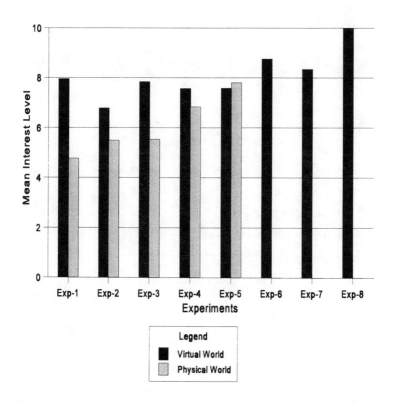

FIGURE 1. Interest level comparison between the tasks performed in the physical world and the virtual world.

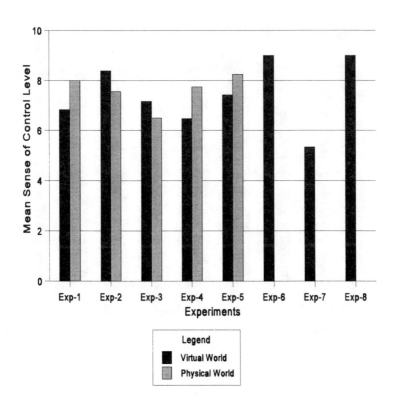

FIGURE 2. Sense of control level comparison between the tasks performed in the physical world and the virtual world.

CHAPTER 9

Safety Issues of VRT

While there are some potential risks associated with virtual environment technology, as pointed out by Stanney (1995), definite steps have been taken in our projects to minimize these risks. According to Stanney, subjects at risk for psychological harm are primarily those who suffer from panic attacks, those with serious medical problems such as heart disease or epilepsy, and those who are (or have recently been) taking drugs with major physiological or psychological effects. As is clearly stated above, questions regarding these situations have been asked as a part of the screening process, and persons with these characteristics have been excluded from serving as subjects in the research projects conducted at CAU. Also, some people experience symptoms ranging from headache to epileptic seizure when exposed to visual stimuli which flicker at 8-12 Hz. In these projects, no frame update rates in this range were used. Furthermore, subjects have been closely observed by experimenters at all times, and if there were evidence of any significant physical or psychological distress, both the subject and the experimenter had the ability to quickly terminate the virtual environment session. We have also increased the frame rate; have asked the patients to sit on a chair rather standing up; have removed the eye-cups from head-mounted display so the patient could see her physical body partially; have chosen the head-mounted display with a narrower field of view; and most importantly have kept the sessions brief (between 20 to 30 minutes). This configuration reduces the degree of immersion but increases the physical and psychological safety of the patients. Given these safeguards, and the fact that no subjects have experienced harm in the previous virtual environment studies at CAU, we feel confident in saying that patient risk in these studies have been minimal and acceptable. There is still a great need for research in this area and we strongly recommend that researchers take appropriate steps in minimizing patient risks.

It must also be noted that symptoms of anxiety while under VRT are distinctly different from simulation sickness. The anxiety symptoms evoked under VRT are the same as the real world experience of the patient and include shortness of breath, heart palpitations (irregular or rapid heartbeat), trembling or shaking, choking, numbness, sweating, dizziness or loss of balance, feeling of detachment, being out of touch with self, hot flashes or chills, loss of control, abdominal distress, and nausea. Below is a paper written by Dr. Kay Stanney providing an in-depth study of human factors in virtual reality. Because of the importance of this subject, we have included the entire paper as an introduction to health and safety issues of virtual reality experiences. Reprinted(©1995 IEEE), with permission, from *Proceedings of Virtual Reality Annual International Symposium '95*, Research Triangle Park, North Carolina, March 1995, 28-34.

Realizing the Full Potential of Virtual Reality: Human Factors Issues That Could Stand in the Way

Kay Stanney, Ph.D.
Industrial Engineering & Management Systems Department
University of Central Florida

ABSTRACT

This paper reviews several significant human factors issues that could stand in the way of virtual reality realizing its full potential. These issues involve maximizing human performance efficiency in virtual environments, minimizing health and safety issues, and circumventing potential social issues through proactive assessment.

INTRODUCTION

Virtual reality technology will be used to advance many fields, including medicine, education, design, training, and entertainment. The reality is, however, a considerable amount of systematic research must be done before virtual reality technology receives widespread use (Kalawsky, 1993). If virtual reality systems are to be effective and well received by their users, researchers need to focus significant efforts on addressing a number of human factors issues (Thomas and Stuart, 1992). This paper provides and overview of many of these human factors issues, including: human performance efficiency in virtual worlds; which is likely influenced by tasks characteristics, user characteristics, human sensory and motor physiology, multi-modal interaction, and the potential need for new design metaphors; health and safety issues, of which cybersickness may pose the most concern; and the social impact of the technology.

HUMAN PERFORMANCE EFFICIENCY IN VIRTUAL WORLDS

Computer speed and functionality, image processing, synthetic sound, and tracking mechanism have been joined together to provide realistic virtual worlds. A fundamental advance still required for virtual environments (VEs) to be effective is to determine how to maximize the efficiency of human task performance in virtual worlds. While it is difficult to gauge the importance of the various human factors issues requiring attention, it is clear that if humans cannot perform efficiently in virtual environments, then further pursuit of this technology may be fruitless. Focusing on understanding how humans can perform most effectively in VEs is thus of primary importance in advancing this technology.

Human performance in VEs will likely be influenced by several factors, including: task characteristic; user characteristics; design constraints imposed by human sensory and motor physiology; integration issues with multi-modal interaction; and the potential need for new visual, auditory and haptic design metaphors uniquely suited to virtual environments.

Task Characteristics

One important aspect that will directly influence how effectively humans can function in virtual worlds is the nature of the tasks being performed. Some tasks may be uniquely suited to virtual representation, while others may not be effectively performed in such environments. It is important to determine the types of tasks for which VEs will be appropriate. In order to obtain this understanding corresponding virtual environment characteristics which effectively support their performance (e.g., stereoscopic 3D visualization, real-time interactivity, immersion, etc.) must be attained.

While there is limited research on the types of task characteristics that are uniquely suited to human-virtual environment interaction (HV-EI) (a notable exception is Wickens and Merwin, 1994), there is extensive literature on tasks which are appropriate for virtual environment training, this body of knowledge on task characteristics must be explored and its relation to virtual task performance needs to be identified. For example, task characteristics which lend themselves to perceptual understanding through three-dimensional visualization in a virtual world should be distinguished. Bennett, Toms and Woods (1993) research supports the use of such 3D displays for tasks requiring information integration. On the other hand, focused attention tasks tend to be more effectively performed using 2D displays. Thus, displaying such tasks in 3D stereoscopic virtual worlds could potentially hinder performance.

Task characteristics which are suitable for representation as displayable virtual objects which can be manipulated through perceptual and motor processes also need to be determined. For example, Sollenberger and Milgram (1993) found optimal path tracking performance when using a 3D, rotating, stereoscopic display. Texturing, the surface rendering available on virtual objects, has been found to be effective for representing additional data dimensions, such as emergent features. These relationships need to be further explored in order to clearly delineate the specific characteristics of virtual worlds which support and enhance task performance as compared to other visualization approaches such as real-time simulations, animations, and non-interactive three-dimensional visualizations.

A taxonomy of virtual task characteristics would be instrumental in providing designers with a tool to guide and direct their design efforts in order to maximize human performance. Such a tool would classify tasks according to the types of information displays (e.g., 2D, 3D stereoscopic, point, line, angle, area, volume, etc.) and interactions (e.g., passive, enactive, interactive) which maximize human-performance efficiency in virtual worlds. The influences of user characteristics (e.g., high versus low spatial individuals) would also need to be considered. Such a taxonomy could assist in guiding VE designers by imposing order (Shneiderman, 1992) on the complex interactions between user, task, and system phenomena.

User Characteristics

An important aspect influencing human VE performance is the affect of user differences. Significantly individual performance differences have already been noted in early studies (Lampton et al, 1994). User characteristics that significantly influence virtual reality experiences need to be identified in order to design virtual reality systems that accommodate the unique needs of users. In order to determine which user characteristics are influential in VEs one can examine studies in human-computer interaction (HCI). In HCI one of the primary user characteristics which interface designers adapt to is level of experience. Experience level influences the skills of the user, the abilities which predict performance, and the manner in which users understand and organize task information (Egan, 1988). In examining the influences of experience on HVEI, one could thus predict that experience would influence the skill with which users interact with the VE and the manner in which uses mentally represent a virtual environment over time. The implication being that designers must design the VE interface to be appropriate for the level of expertise of the target user population. Understanding what is an "appropriate" VE interface for novices versus experts is a challenge.

Technical aptitudes (e.g., spatial visualization, orientation, spatial memory, spatial scanning) are generally significant in predicting HCI performance (Egan, 1988). These studies indicate that individuals who score low on spatial memory tests generally have longer mean execution times and more tests generally have longer mean execution times and more first try errors. These studies also suggest that the difficulties experienced by low spatial individuals are particularly related to system navigation issues—users often report being "lost" within hierarchical menu systems (Sellen and Nicol, 1990). These findings are particularly relevant to VEs which may often place a high demand on navigation skills. In fact, users are already know to become lost in virtual worlds (McGovern, 1993). The issue is thus how to assist low spatial users with maintaining spatial orientation within virtual worlds. New design metaphors could potentially be developed to assist with this issue.

Other aptitudes, such as verbal and motor ability, and traits, such as personality, that have not been found to consistently predict human computer performance (Egan, 1988), may become more influential during HVEI. Particularly with the emphasis on audio and haptic interaction modes in VEs (Kalawsky, 1993; Larijani, 1994), it is essential that human factors analysis be devoted to understanding the influences of these other aptitudes on HVEI.

Design Constraints Imposed by Human Sensory and Motor Physiology

In order for designers to be able to maximize human efficiency in VEs in it is essential to obtain an understanding of design constraints imposed by human sensory and motor physiology. Without a foundation of knowledge in these areas there is a chance that the multi-modal interactions provided by VE systems will not be compatible with their users. Such design incompatibilities could place artificial limits on human VE performance. VE design requirements and constraints aimed at maximizing human VE performance should thus be developed by taking into consideration the abilities and limitations of humans (Kalawsky, 1993). The physiological and perceptual issues which directly impact the design of multi-modal VEs, include: visual perception, auditory perception, and haptic perception.

Visual Perception

The design of visual presentations for VEs is complicated because the human visual system is very sensitive to any anomalies in perceived imagery, especially in motion scenes (Larijani, 1994). During virtual motion scenes, minute, nearly imperceptible scene anomalies become dreadfully apparent because of the unnatural appearance of visual flow field cues (Kalawsky, 1993). In order to avoid this issue, more research is needed to develop guidelines that assist designers in fabricating approximate optical flow patterns. In general, human visual perception needs to be better understood in order to ensure that the most effective visual scenes are developed for virtual worlds.

It is also important to determine what a viewer can see in a VE, that is to determine the viewer's visual field when wearing a Head Mounted Display (HMD). In order to determine exactly what individuals can see in HMDs, visual field graphical dimensions must be overlaid onto obscuration plots imposed by HMDs. HMDs substantially reduce the field of view (FOV) of a user, thus obscuring the perception of motion in the peripheral vision. Current systems are generally limited to a FOV of 70 degrees per eye and do not provide peripheral vision (Larijani, 1994). Kalawsky (1993) has suggested, but not yet proven, that many virtual tasks will require FOVs of 100 degrees or more in order to achieve immersive environments. These suggestions needed to be further studies in order to determine what FOV is required to perform different kinds of virtual tasks effectively. Then the extent to which FOVs need to be enlarged can be specified.

Auditory Perception

In order to synthesize a realistic auditory environment it is important to obtain a better understanding of how the ears receive sound, particularly focusing on 3-D audio localization. Although it is known that audio localization is primarily determined by intensity differences and temporal or phase differences between signals at the ears, such localization is affected by the presence of other sounds and the direction from which these sounds originate (Kalawsky, 1993). In addition, while auditory localization is understood in the horizontal plane (left to right), localization in the median plane (intersection between front and back) and discrimination of sounds from front to back are not well understood. Thus, much work is needed in order to effectively synthesize 3D auditory environments.

In order to study 3-D audio localization, binaural localization cues received by the ears can be represented by a Head Related Transfer Function (HRTF), phase differences, and overtones (Cohen, 1992). The HRTF represents the manner in which sound sources change as a listener moves his/her head can be specified with knowledge of the source position and the position and orientation of the head. Personalized HRTFs may need to be developed because these functions are dependent on the physiological makeup of each individual listener's ear. Ideally, a more generalized HRTF could be designed that would be applicable to a multitude of users.

Haptic Perception

A haptic sensation (i.e., touch) is a mechanical contact with the skin (Kalawsky, 1993). Three mechanical stimuli produce the sensation of touch: a displacement of the skin over an extended period of time; a transitory (few milliseconds) displacement of the skin; and a transitory displacement of the skin which is repeated at a constant or variable frequency. Even with this understanding of global mechanisms, however, the attributes of the skin area difficult to characterize in a quantitative fashion. This is due to the fact that the skin has variable thresholds for touch (vibrotactile thresholds) and can perform complex spatial and temporal summations which are all a function of the type and position of the mechanical stimuli. So as the stimulus changes so does the sensation of touch, thus creating a challenge for those attempting to model synthetic haptic feedback.

Another haptic issue is that the sensations of the skin adapt with exposure to a stimuli. More specifically, the effect of a sensation decreases in sensitivity to a continued stimulus, may disappear completely even though the stimulus is still present, and varies by receptor type. Surface characteristics of the stimulus (e.g., hard, soft, textured) also influence the sensation of touch.

In order to communicate the sensation of synthetic remote touch it is thus essential to have an understanding of: the mechanical stimuli which produce the sensation of touch; the vibrotactile thresholds; the effect of a sensation; the dynamic range of the touch receptors; and the adaptation of these receptors to certain types of stimuli. The human haptic system needs to be more fully characterized, potentially through a computational model of the physical properties of the skin, in order to generate synthesized haptic responses.

Integration Issues with Multi-Modal Interaction

While developers are focusing on synthesizing effective visual, auditory, and haptic representations in virtual worlds, it is also important to determine how to effectively integrate this multi-modal interaction. One of the aspects that makes VEs unique from other interactive technologies is its ability to present the user with multiple inputs and outputs. This multi-modal interaction may be a primary factor that leads to enhanced human performance for certain tasks presented in virtual worlds. Early studies have already indicated that sensorial redundancy can enhance human performance in virtual worlds Massimino and Sheridan, 1993). There is currently, however, a limited understanding on how to effectively provide such sensorial parallelism (Burdea and Coiffet, 1994). When sensorial redundancy is provided to users it is essential to consider the design of the integration of these multiple sources of feedback. One means of addressing this integration issue is to consider (1) the coordination between sensing and user command and (2) the transposition of senses in the feedback loop.

Command coordination considers the user input as primarily mono-modal (e.g., through gesture or voice) and feedback to the user as multi-modal (i.e., any combination of visual, auditory, and/or haptic). There is limited understanding on such issues as (1) is there any need for redundant user input (e.g., voice and direct manipulation used to activate the same action); (2) can users effectively handle parallel input (e.g., select an object with a mouse at the same time as directing a search via voice input); and (3) for which tasks is voice input most appropriate, gesture most appropriate, and direct manipulation most appropriate.

Sensorial transposition occurs when a user receives feedback through other senses than those expected. This may occur because a VE designer's command coordination scheme has substituted unavailable system sensory feedback (e.g., force feedback) with other modes of feedback (e.g. visual or auditory). Such substitution has been found to be feasible (e.g., Massimino and Sheridan, 1993) successfully substituted vibrotactile and auditory feedback for force feedback in a peg-in-hole task). VE designers thus need to establish the most effective sensorial transposition schemes for their virtual tasks. The design of these substitutions schemes should be consistent throughout the virtual world to avoid sensorial confusion.

Virtual Environment Design Metaphors

It is known that well-designed metaphors can assist novice users in effectively performing tasks in human-computer interaction (Carrol and Mack, 1985). Thus, designing effective VE metaphors could similarly enhance human performance in virtual worlds. Such metaphors may also be a means of assisting in the integration of multi-modal interaction. For example, affordances may be designed that assist users in interacting with the virtual world much as they would interact with the multi-modal real world.Unfortunately, at the present time many human-VE interface designers are using old metaphors (e.g., windows, toolbars), that may be inappropriate for HVEI.

Oren (1990) suggested that every new technology goes through an initial incunabular stage, where old forms continue to exist which may not be suited to the new medium. Currently, virtual technology appears to be in such a stage. For example, many users of virtual environments don their high tech helmet and gloves and enter the virtual world only to find floating menus awaiting them! Virtual environments are in need of new design metaphors uniquely suited to their characteristics and requirements.

McDowell (1994) has suggested that the design of interface metaphors may prove to be the most challenging area in VE development. VR sliders (3D equivalents of scroll bars), map cubes (3D maps which show space in a viewer's vicinity), and tow planes (where a viewer's navigation is tied to a virtual object which tow him/her about the VE) are all being investigated as potential visual metaphors for virtual environments.

Beyond the need for new visual metaphors, VEs may also need auditory metaphors which provide a means of effectively presenting auditory information to users. Cohen (1992) has provided some insight into potential auditory metaphors through the development of "multidimensional audio windows" or MAW. MAW provides a conceptual model for organizing and controlling sound within traditional window-icon-menu-pointing device (WIMP) interfaces. In addition, Hahn, Gritz, Darken, Geigel and Won Lee (1993) have developed the concept of 'timbre trees' which are general timbre trees can be used as a construction methodology for representing any new synthetic sound.

Metaphors for haptic interaction may also be required. Limited work has been done in this area to date and no noted haptic metaphors have been presented.

HEALTH AND SAFETY ISSUES IN VIRTUAL ENVIRONMENTS

Maximizing human performance in VEs in essential to the success of this technology. Of equal importance is ensuring the health and welfare of users who interact with these environments. If the human element in these systems is ignored or minimized it could result in discomfort, harm, or even injury. It is essential that VE developers ensure that advances in VE technology do not come at the cost of human well being.

There are several health and safety issues which may affect users of VEs. These issues include both direct and indirect affects (Viirre, 1994). The direct effects can be looked at from a microscopic level (e.g., individual tissue) or a macroscopic level (e.g., trauma). The indirect effects are primarily psychological.

There are several microscopic direct effects which could affect the tissues of VE users. The eyes, which will be closely coupled to HMDs or other visual displays used in VEs, have the potential of being harmed. The central nervous system (CNS) could be affected by the emfs of VE systems.

Some individuals are susceptible to "flicker vertigo"—when they are exposed to flickering lights (usually in the range of 8 to 12 Hz) they experience a seizure. VE displays flickering at this rate could lead to seizure in a few users, even in some unaware that they have the condition.

Phobic effects may result from VE use, such as claustrophobia (e.g., HMD enclosure) and anxiety (e.g., falling of a cliff in a virtual world). Viirre (1994) suggests, but has yet to prove, that no long term phobic effects should result from HVEI, except potential avoidance of VE exposure.

The auditory system and inner ear could be adversely affected by VE exposure to high volume audio (e.g., the "Walkman" effect). One of the possible affects of such exposure is noise induced hearing loss. Prolonged repetitive VE movements could also cause overuse injuries to the body (e.g., carpal tunnel syndrome, tenosynovitis, epicondylitis). The head, neck and spine could be harmed by the weight or position of HMDs (Kalawsky, 1993; Viirre, 1994).

Limited or eliminated vision of natural surroundings when wearing HMDs could lead to falls or trips that result in bumps and bruises. Sound cues may distract users causing them to fall while viewing virtual scenes. Imbalance of body position may occur due to the weight of VE equipment or tethers that link equipment to computers causing users to fall (Thomas and Stuart, 1992). Obstacles in the real world, that may not be visible in the virtual world, could pose a threat to the safety of users. If haptic feedback systems fail a user might be accidentally pinched, pulled or otherwise harmed. Another direct macroscopic effect that could prevent virtual reality from realizing its full potential is that many users of VEs experience motion sickness (i.e., cybersickness). Such sickness may prevent users from seeking further VE interactions.

The use of VEs may produce disturbing after-effects, such as head spinning and delayed onset of sickness. Delayed effects from virtual experiences must be investigated in order to ensure the safety of users once interaction with a virtual world concludes.

If a system fails, the sudden disruption of "presence" may cause disorientation, discomfort, and/or harm. Finally, psychological or emotional well-being could be negatively influenced by VE interaction (e.g., addiction, transfer-of-training from violent VEs). All of these health and safety issues must be addressed in order to ensure the well being of users interacting with virtual worlds.

Cybersickness

One of the most important health and safety issues that may influence the advancement of VE technology is cybersickness.Cybersickness (CS) is a form of motion sickness that occurs as a result of exposure to VEs. Cybersickness poses a serious threat to the usability of VE systems. Users of VE systems generally experience various levels of sickness ranging from headaches to severe nausea (Kalawsky, 1993). Although there are many suggestions about the causes of motion sickness, to date there are no definitive theories of cybersickness. Research needs to be done in order to identify the specific causes of CS and their interrelationships in order to develop methods which alleviate this malady. If CS is not adequately addressed, many individuals may avert VE experiences in order to avoid becoming sick.

Motion sickness is considered to be the product of a cue conflict acting upon the visual and/or vestibular systems (Hettinger, et al, 1990). The user's body perceives this conflict as a poison and attempts to remove this "poison" by making itself sick (Money and Cheung, 1983). Motion sickness may manifest itself in the form of headaches, blurred vision, salivation, burping, eye strain, dizziness, vertigo, disorientation, or even severe vomiting. It has been shown that between 10 to 60% of users demonstrate some form of simulator sickness (Kennedy, Fowlkes and Hettinger, 1989). For those who do become sick, research has shown that CS may prevent a person from wanting to reenter a virtual world (Barfield and Weghorst, 1993). Currently, however, system developers cannot prevent such sickness from occurring because the exact causes of motion sickness are not well defined.

While it is known that users adapt to VE experiences and become less sick over time (Held and Durlach, 1993), the first impressions of users may influence their attitudes towards this technology. If users become very ill during their initial experience, they may avoid future VE interactions. Relying on adaptation alone as a remedy for CS may thus not prove effective.

There have been several studies focused on understanding the factors that may contribute to motion sickness (e.g., vection, lag, field of view, etc.), yet no general theory of motion sickness has resulted from this research. In fact, contradictory evidence among the existing studies leads to skepticism about the actual impact of each of these factors. The reason for these contradictions may be due to the fact that in some of these studies users were in control of their moment about the simulated world, while in other they were confined to a predestined course. Control may provide users with a means of adapting to or accommodating cue conflicts by building conditioned expectations through repeated interactions with a virtual world (e.g., when a user's head turns the user learns to expect the world to follow milliseconds behind). Lack of control would not be aware of which way they were turning at any particular moment (i.e., the course would be determined by the system). Thus, without control, users would not be expected to adapt to cue conflicts. User control in conjunction with adaptation may provide a means of minimizing the influences of cybersickness.

Research on CS needs to be conducted in order to fully specify the relationships between control, adaptation, and CS. Control also needs to be tested against varying degrees of other factors to see what level of freedom is necessary to potentially negate their affects. The research should focus on developing a general theory of CS which would allow for the prediction of the combinations of factors which would be disruptive and lead to CS; those which would be easy or hard to adapt to; and the relationship of these levels of adaptation to the level of user control. Such a theory would provide VE developers with the knowledge necessary to minimize the adverse effects of VE interaction.

THE SOCIAL IMPACT OF VIRTUAL TECHNOLOGY

While researchers are often concerned about the human performance and health and safety issues when developing a new technology, an often times neglected effect of new technologies is their potential social impact. Virtual reality is a technology, which like its ancestors (e.g., television, computers, video games) has the potential for negative social implications through misuse and abuse (Kallman, 1993). Its higher level of user interaction may even pose a greater threat than past technologies. Through a careful analysis, some of the problems of VEs may be anticipated and perhaps prevented. A proactive, rather than reactive, approach may allow researchers to identify and address potentially harmful side-effects related to the use of VE technology. Such an approach requires that researchers and developers prioritize social issues early on in VE development, rather than taking a wait-and-see attitude. Most virtual reality conferences have yet to even recognize and address that social issues may exits.

Currently the potential negative social influences resulting from VE exposure are not well understood. There are many open issues (Kallman, 1993; Sheridan, 1993; Stone, 1993; Whiteback, 1993), such as: What will be the psychological and character effects of VE use? How will interaction in the virtual world modify behavior? What will the 'transfer of training' be for violent virtual interactions? Will individuals transfer violent virtual experiences to the real world? Will people turn their backs on the real world and become "contented zombies" wandering around synthetic worlds which fulfill their whims but disregard their growth as a human being? Will virtual reality users experience traumatic physical or psychological consequences due to a virtual interaction? Will people avoid reality and real social encounters with peers and become addicted to escapism? Is continual exposure to violent virtual worlds similar to military training, which through continued exposure may desensitize individuals to the acts of killing and maiming? Could the behaviors of soldiers after intense military training events provide an indication of the influences of intense violent VE interactions? How will VE influence young children who are particularly liable to psychological and moral influence? Does VE raise issues which are genuinely novel over past media due to the salience of the experience and the active interaction of the user? These issues need to be proactively explored in order to circumvent negative social consequences from HVEI.

CONCLUSIONS

This paper has presented many of the human factors issues which must be addressed in order for virtual reality technology to reach its full potential without inflicting harm along the way. Virtual reality technology promises to permeate both professional and personal aspects of our lives. If this influx is to be a positive influence rather than a forceful intrusion, it is essential that each of these human factors issues receive significant systematic research.

❖   ❖   ❖

The Nature of
Virtual Presence in VRT

INTRODUCTION

One of the major attributes of virtual reality is the sense of presence (virtual presence) that users experience while immersed in a virtual reality scene. Our basic understanding of virtual presence, however, is still primarily anecdotal in nature. There is a great need to rigorously explore the basic questions concerning the nature of virtual presence. Several innovative experiments using virtual reality to combat psychological disorders have been described in this book. In these experiments, the sense of virtual presence was the defining factor that resulted in successful outcomes and provided the authors with experimental evidence upon which to formulate several assertions about the characteristics and nature of virtual presence.

Thus, we have conducted several experiments in virtual environments as a way to identify and explore issues related to the concept of *sense of presence* (what we term "virtual presence", including telepresence, to distinguish it from physical presence; for convenience, these terms may be used interchangeably: presence and virtual presence). In the first set of experiments, virtual environment desensitization (VED) was utilized to treat subjects who suffered from agoraphobia., VED was used as an alternative and potentially more effective and efficient approach to treating agoraphobia compared to in vivo treatment, a gradual exposure of the subject to phobic situations in the real world, (North and North, 1994; North, North, and Coble, 1995a, 1995b, 1996a, 1996b, 1996c, 1997). We have also conducted several other experiments to investigate the effectiveness of virtual reality technology in motivating learners (North, 1996a, 1996b). Virtual presence and physical presence were compared in a target detection training situation (North, Swift and Raglin, 1995 unpublished).

A number of articles have been published recently on the experience of *presence* in a virtual or remote environment. Sheridan (1992) proposed three measurable physical variables that determine presence: extent of sensory information, control of relationship of sensors to environment, and ability to modify physical environment. Both Naiman (1992) and Loomis (1992) have argued that the normal human experience is not of the physical world but of our perceptions of the physical world. That is, reality is what we perceive it to be. In his taxonomy of graphics simulation systems, Zeltzer (1992), identified presence with the number and fidelity of available sensory input and output channels. Heeter (1992) discussed three dimensions—personal, social and environmental—of the subjective experience of presence.Fontaine (1992), based on analysis of international and inter-cultural encounters, identified a sense of presence with a state of consciousness in which one experiences "realness, vividness, and feeling very much alive," "attending to the immediate situation," "a perception of thinking and acting in new and innovative ways," and "a broad awareness of everything around." Held and Durlach (1992) discussed the need to define sensorimotor and cognitive factors that determine a sense of presence. Mowafy, Russo and Miller (1993) investigated the role of presence in training tasks involving construction of mental models of spatial relationships.Pausch, Shackelford and Proffit (1993) have demonstrated a generic search task in which users perform better in an immersive environment than in a stationary display window.

As pointed out by several authors(Held and Durlach,1992; Sheridan, 1992; Kalawsky, 1993), we have not yet developed a scientific body of knowledge or theory delineating the factors underlying the phenomenon of virtual presence. There is, however, an emerging general consensus within the virtual environments and teleoperations community on several issues that are important to the development and scientific use of the concept of virtual presence. Based on the literature and our own experiences there are many open questions concerning virtual presence in virtual environment situations. We introduce a few of these questions here and attempt to answer them empirically either individually or collectively.

(1)   Is there a sufficiently useful operational and quantitative definition of virtual presence?

(2)   How can virtual presence be quantified?

(3)   What are the factors that create virtual presence?

(4)   Is there any relationship between virtual presence and subject performance?

(5)   What is the difference between virtual presence and physical presence, and is there a relationship between the two?

On the following pages we attempt to provide answers to these questions. Based on the collected data from the VRT experiments and our observations of subjects' behavior, we make several assertions concerning the sense of virtual presence.

ASSERTIONS CONCERNING VIRTUAL PRESENCE

Based on the data collected and subjects' verbal reports of the experiments we make these assertions concerning the sense of virtual presence:

- *A person's experience of a situation in a virtual environment may evoke the same reactions and emotions as the experience in a similar real-world situation.*

All of our research studies of psychological treatment categories demonstrated that people who are agoraphobic in the real world are also agoraphobic in a virtual world. When subjected to virtual phobic-invoking situations, our subjects exhibited the same types of responses as would be exhibited in a real-world situation. These responses included anxiety, avoidance, and physical symptoms.

As a measure of anxiety, subjects were repeatedly asked to rate their current level of anxiety on a SUD scale. The relatively high SUD scores at the beginning of each treatment session indicated that the subjects' fear structures were invoked and the SUD scores (and thus fear levels) gradually decreased as subjects remained in the virtual scene.

A second measure of anxiety was subject behavior and verbalization. Examples of common subject behavior included tightly gripping the rails and displaying reluctance to let go of the rails. These are some of the verbal expressions we recorded: "The higher I get, the more worried I get." "I am really there!" "It feels like being in a real helicopter." "I am afraid to fall down!" "I do not like this at all!" "I am scared!" "I feel like I am actually on the fiftieth floor!"

Physical symptoms reported by subjects included shakiness in the knees, heart palpitations, tenseness, sweaty palms, and dizziness.

- *A person may experience a sense of virtual presence similar to the real world even when the virtual environment does not accurately or completely represent the real-world situation.*

Remarkably, subject reactions consistent with phobic stimuli were experienced in spite of the fact that their virtual experience did not correspond to the real-world experience in several ways. All visual environments were much less detailed than a real scene would have been, and some environments included much simpler auditory and tactile cues, such as engine sound and vibration designed to approximate the Apache AH64 helicopter in the fear of flying study.

As stated previously, the subjects reported a number of physical and emotional anxiety-related symptoms such as dizziness, sweaty palms, and heart palpitations. These feelings would not have been reported by the subjects if they had not perceived that they were experiencing a realistic situation, even though the virtual environments were far from being exact copies of real world scenes.

- *Each person brings her own background into a virtual reality experience.*

It is important to recognize that perception is in many ways just as much a product of our previous experiences as of current stimulation. Each subject is a unique, special individual with an independent experience of reality that is unique and different from the objective world, or the so-called world of reality. The implication for virtual environments is that the sense of virtual presence is dependent not only on the physical qualities (resolution, realism, interactivity, lag time, etc.) of the experience provided by the virtual environment, but also upon what the participant psychologically brings to the environment. The very nature of perception causes each person to react differently to the same real or virtual experience.

This was evidenced by SUD and ATAQ scores and the verbal comments of the subjects. Just as various individuals may react differently to a real world experience, our subjects exhibited different reactions to the same virtual world experience. This point was clearly demonstrated by the variety of responses among subjects to the same phobic stimuli in the virtual scene.Several subjects went through several levels of phobic situations without reporting any significant anxiety. On the other hand, many subjects reported differing amounts of anxiety at different levels of the virtual scene. There was major variation in the amount of time subjects spent in each level of the virtual scenes.

- *Experience with a virtual environment increases the participant's sense of virtual presence.*

The idea that a sense of virtual presence may increase with experience has been suggested by several researchers (Naiman, 1992; Held and Durlach, 1992; Loomis, 1992, 1993).Our experiments verified this hypothesis, in that the longer subjects stayed in the virtual scene the deeper they were pulled into the virtual world and the greater their sense of virtual presence.

Based on SUD and ATAQ scores and verbal comments during the experiments, most subjects initially felt some level of virtual presence in the phobic situation and their sense of virtual presence increased over time, or at least was maintained during all the sessions.

- *The sense of presence in virtual and physical environments is constant. Subjects have to give up the sense of presence in a physical environment in order to achieve a stronger sense of presence in the virtual one.*

This assertion is based on the data drawn from SPSVP (Sense of Presence Scale in Virtual and Physical environments) and SUD questionnaires. The SPSVP was designed to assess one's sense of presence in the virtual and physical environments, sense of interactivity with the virtual environment system, and perception of the real world as reflected in the virtual environment.

The subjective measures of sense of presence in the virtual environment increased gradually during each session. The subjective measures of sense of presence of the physical environment while in the virtual environment decreased gradually within and between sessions. These results led to the conclusion that the longer subjects remained in the virtual environment the higher was the sense of presence in the virtual environment (even when using very minimal stimuli), while the sense of presence of the physical environment decreased. This supports a theory that the total sense of presence is constant, and subjects have to divide their overall sense of presence between the virtual and real worlds.

- *Subject concentration increases significantly in the virtual world as compared to the physical world when the subject has enough interaction to develop a strong sense of virtual presence.*

Each subject's interest level in the learning study was determined by a ten-point scale instrument administered at the end of each experiment. The scores ranged from very weak to very strong. The interest level and sense of control level in the virtual world were always higher than the scores in the physical world.

Based on the data and observation, it was obvious that each subject was excited, enthusiastic, and eager to be in the virtual environment rather than the physical environment. The main conclusion of this research was that memory span increased significantly in the virtual environment as compared to the span in the physical environment, and that the learner's motivation and interest levels may be maintained longer in the virtual environment. We hypothesize that at least a part of this effect may be due to the simplicity of the virtual environment, providing less distractions to the learner.

- *A person's perceptions of real-world situations and behavior in the real-world may be modified based on her experiences within a virtual world.*

Most applications of virtual reality are intended to augment human intelligence by either increasing or modifying a person's *intellectual understanding* of the structure or nature of objects or tasks (Bajura, et al, 1992). A virtual environment can also modify users' perceptions of real world situations and thus behavior in those situations.

This conclusion is based on the reports of subjects who exposed themselves to real world phobic situations after receiving VED treatment. What was learned and experienced in the virtual environment was transferred to real-world perception and behavior.

CONCLUSION AND DISCUSSION

We now return to our list of open questions concerning *virtual presence.* Our purpose is not to completely resolve the questions but to suggest some answers and intellectually excite other researchers to conduct experiments in order to more systematically analyze and study this most important factor of virtual environment, the sense of virtual presence.

(1)   Is there a sufficiently useful operational and quantitative definition of virtual presence?

The answer to this question is mixed. Useful? Yes. Operational? No. Quantitative? Yes, with some qualification.

A number of definitions of presence have been offered in the literature. The definition that we introduce is a variation of the definition offered by Sheridan (1992).

Virtual Presence is <u>the perception of being physically present</u> in a computer generated or remote environment.

Our basic assertion in this definition is in agreement with that of Loomis (1993) that "the phenomenology of synthetic experience is continuous with that of ordinary experience." While this assertion may at first appear rather trivial, it is, in fact, of extreme importance. Those subjects who appear to become the most immersed in virtual environments (and who often benefit the most from such exposures) frequently are heard to make comments such as these: "This is just like the real thing," or "I'm really getting up there now." With a strong sense of virtual presence, the subject is not merely being entertained by a nice computer game but has entered an alternate world, which is assumed to operate under the same set of rules as the real world.

Unfortunately, the acceptance of such a definition recognizes sense of virtual presence as a perception, a private experience that cannot be readily defined in operational terms. This does not, however, mean that sense of virtual presence cannot be quantified. Self-report scales, while always subject to question, can certainly yield quantitative data; and our experience has been that these reports show significant reliability and validity.

(2)   What are the factors that create virtual presence?

In the spirit of previous models by Zeltzer (1992) and Sheridan (1992), we present our own three-axis taxonomy of a *sense of virtual presence*. A participant's sense of virtual presence in an environment may be represented by three primary determinants:

1. *Fidelity and extent of sensory information.* This axis corresponds closely to the "sensory information" axis proposed by Sheridan (1992) or the "presence" axis proposed by Zeltzer (1992) and can be measured with respect to the quality and quantity of information that is available to a person experiencing a virtual environment.

2. *Participant's interaction.* This axis corresponds to the interaction between a participant and the environment. On a basic level it would include the ability of a participant to modify his point of view through head movement, or to interact with objects (or other participants) in the environment.

3. *Previous life experience of the participant.* This axis represents the existential world (or personal reality) which the participant brings to the virtual environment, in the sense that a person's perception is not merely a reaction to the present sensory environment, but also an interpretation of that environment in light of all the individual's previous experiences.

Figure 1 illustrates these three determinants of virtual presence as orthogonal axes of a Stimulus, Interaction and Experience (SIE) cube. We postulate that a sense of virtual presence may be associated with every point inside the cube. The intensity or vigor of the sense of virtual presence would, in general, increase as we move along each axis. Our understanding of virtual presence differs from previous models in several respects. Previous taxonomies have ignored the notion of experience as a primary determinant of the nature and intensity of a user's sense of virtual presence for a given situation or task.Our work with agoraphobic subjects and other subjects has clearly illustrated that what the user psychologically brings to the environment is important to her perception of the environment and can not be ignored.

(3)   How can virtual presence be quantified?

At first glance, this would appear to be a difficult task, since virtual presence is a subjective experience.It has been our experience, however, that subjective measures of virtual presence are highly reliable and valid, a conclusion supported by Thyer et al (1984). Their study showed a high correlation between subjective measures and physiological measures of arousal.

(4)   Is there any relationship between virtual presence and subject performance?

This is an area that needs more extensive exploration, but the question can be answered with a reasonably strong "yes." While quantitative data is limited, we have gained the strong impression in a variety of situations that subjects with the greatest virtual presence also tend to perform best and improve most in the virtual environments.

(5)   What is the difference between virtual presence and physical presence, and is there a relationship between the two?

   As mentioned above, we have explored this question directly, finding that there is a strong negative correlation between virtual presence and physical presence. Our current hypothesis is that there is basically a fixed total amount of presence, which can either be devoted totally to the physical world, devoted totally to the virtual world, or split between the two. Such a hypothesis seems consistent with our common experience with standard media, where serious immersion in a book or movie is often accompanied by decreased awareness of physical stimuli from the real world.

   In conclusion, while there is certainly much work to be done in exploring the phenomenon of virtual presence, we are well on our way to answering many of the most basic questions in this area. With the strong resemblance between virtual presence and physical presence, it appears certain that virtual environments will soon move far beyond the arcade, because many forms of learning, training, and therapy can be performed much more quickly, easily, economically, and/or safely in the virtual world than in the real world.

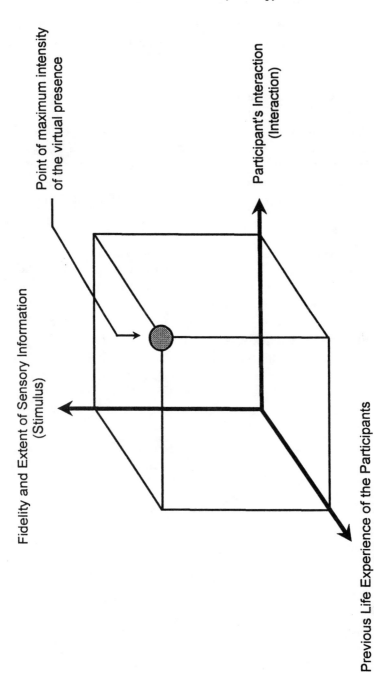

FIGURE 1. The Stimulus, Interaction and Experience (SIE) cube.

CHAPTER 11

Ongoing Research: VRT Combating Other Psychological Disorders

Although results of the research projects covered in this book are impressive, additional research is needed to more thoroughly explore the effectiveness of VRT and extend it to other psychological disorders. Additional studies must allow for both objective and subjective measurements of anxiety to ensure the validity of research outcomes. We recommend investigating the influence of subject variables (demographic and personality characteristics) on the effectiveness of VRT. Such studies should include an imaginal systematic desensitization (ISD) conventional therapy group in addition to the no-treatment control group used in previous studies. In this chapter, we present current and ongoing research in those areas, hoping it will be both informative and inspiring.

These projects include using virtual reality therapy to combat fear of public speaking, obsessive-compulsive disorders (OCD), attention deficit disorders (ADD), post-traumatic stress disorders (PTSD), use of augmented reality to treat Parkinson's disease, and Internet-mediated visualization in behavior therapy by using VRML (virtual reality modeling language).

FEAR OF PUBLIC SPEAKING

Overview

Research into this widespread phobia is being conducted by way of collaboration between the CAU Computer & Information Science and Psychology Departments, U.S. Army Research Laboratory, Boeing Computer Services and the Speech Improvement Company, Inc., a private sector partner in the establishment of a new modality for the treatment of fear of pubic speaking. This research may have far-reaching benefits. It will permit the transfer of this technology to clinical situations through the Speech Improvement Company. The general population will benefit from greater access to a safe, confidential and economical approach to the treatment of psychological disorders that the new technology makes possible.

Goals

Extending VRT Treatment to Fear of Public Speaking

While the results of research projects conducted at CAU and elsewhere have consistently been positive, the kinds of phobias and numbers of subjects treated so far have been limited. This ongoing research project has the potential of significantly increasing the range of the psychological disorders that can be treated with VRT and, in turn, enhancing the significance of the findings.

Objective Measures of Anxiety

One possible criticism of the results of VRT studies at CAU and elsewhere is that the measures of anxiety involved have been primarily, and often exclusively, subjective. There is evidence to suggest that subjective measures of anxiety (more specifically, ratings on the Subjective Units of Disturbance scale) correlate highly with objective measures of anxiety (Thyer et al, 1984). This evidence will be specifically evaluated in this study, where simultaneous subjective and objective measures of anxiety are obtained.

Traditional Therapy (Individual Systematic Desensitization) Control Group

While the VRT studies at CAU and elsewhere have shown significant reductions in the anxiety levels among subjects with phobic disorders, these studies have only included no-treatment control groups, and thus have left open the question of the effectiveness of VRT when compared to traditional individual systematic desensitization (ISD) treatment. This study will include an ISD control group in addition to a no-treatment control group (with sufficient funding). This will make the important additional comparison possible. It should be noted that there is evidence to expect that these two methods may prove to be comparable in effectiveness. In preliminary studies at CAU in which the anxiety and avoidance scales of the Acrophobia Questionnaire were used, the pretreatment scores of subjects were comparable to those seen by Cohen (1977). More importantly, the anxiety and avoidance scores of Cohen's subjects decreased by 28.6 and 6.7, respectively, while the CAU decreases were 37.3 and 13.3.

Follow-Up

A final possible criticism of previous studies is the question of whether or not any anxiety reductions seen in the laboratory translate to more adaptive behavior in the real world. A final extension of current research data provided by this study will be an attempt to evaluate changes which have occurred in the subjects' everyday lives. An evaluation will be conducted at least one month after the completion of VRT or ISD treatment. Further evaluation of the changes will be conducted as indicated by the data and the availability of funding. Such measures will add additional significance to the data which indicate that VRT is a promising alternative to traditional ISD treatment of phobic disorders.

Specific Objectives And Methods

Subjects

Subjects for the research will be recruited from introductory psychology classes at Clark Atlanta University. At least 15 of the undergraduates will undergo an extensive two-stage screening process to ensure that they are suffering from fear of public speaking, and that they do not have any other serious physical or psychological conditions. The participation of all subjects will be strictly voluntary.

The first stage of the screening process will consist of a set of questionnaires administered in the psychology classes. The questionnaires will contain items that screen students for a circumscribed fear of public speaking consistent with the diagnosis of specific phobia (American Psychiatric Association, 1994). The questionnaires will exclude subjects with panic conditions and other specific disorders including substance disorders, major medical illness including thyroid disease, and use of medication with significant psychotropic or physiologic effects. Additional screening criteria to be included in the questionnaires will be symptom duration of at least one year and strong motivation toward overcoming phobia.

The second phase of the screening process will involve a more stringent diagnostic procedure. It will include a clinical interview and completion of the Hopkins Symptom Checklist (Derogatis, et al, 1974), the Zung Anxiety Scale (Zung, 1971), the Beck Depression Inventory (Beck et al, 1961), and a modified Attitude Towards Public Speaking Questionnaire (Abelson and Curtis, 1989). Subjects having symptoms limited to fear of public speaking (social phobia) and consistent with the diagnosis of specific phobia will be included in the study. During this phase subjects will also complete a questionnaire regarding various demographic variables (sex, geographical region, rural vs. urban, socioeconomic status, experience with computers, computer games and/or virtual reality, etc.). After securing consent from the subjects, the 16 Personality Factors test (16PF) will be administered to each subject. This test will be used because it is widely used, readily available, quick and easy to administer and objectively scored.

The remaining subjects will be assigned to three treatment conditions: imaginal systematic desensitization (ISD), virtual reality therapy (VRT), and a control group. The three groups will be as closely matched as possible with respect to demographic and personality characteristics and severity of symptoms. In order to minimize the confounding variable of treatment expectancy, informed consent for treatment will be obtained after group assignment. After the first set of assigned measures, the control group subjects will be informed that they will undergo repeated testing at the end of the fourth week (expectancy questionnaire), the eighth week, and the twelfth week. All subjects will be asked not to communicate with other subjects and not to self-treat with relaxation upon phobic situation exposure. All subjects will also be asked to keep a diary of new medication regimens, including over-the-counter medications, caffeine use, significant stresses, and new illness and/or treatment.

Assessment Measures

The screening questionnaire used in this study will assess several inclusion and exclusion criteria. DSM-IV criteria for specific phobia (i.e., fear of public speaking, avoidance of feared situations, belief that the fear is excessive, interference from fear), desire for treatment, desire to participate in a treatment study, presence of panic attacks, history of panic attacks, and presence of claustrophobia will be assessed by this instrument.

The **Attitude Towards Public Speaking Questionnaire** (a modified version) contains six items that assess attitudes toward fear of public speaking. It is adapted from Abelson and Curtis (1989). The following dimensions, rated on a 0-10 semantic differential scale: good-bad, awful-nice, pleasant-unpleasant, safe-dangerous, threatening-nonthreatening, and harmful-harmless are included.

The **Fear Questionnaire** will be constructed for use in this study. Included will be the Marks and Mathews' (1979) Fear Questionnaire which assesses the degree of distress experienced from the fear of public speaking. Four situations that subjects will be exposed to are speaking in an auditorium without any audience; speaking in an auditorium with a younger audience; speaking to an audience of peers; or speaking to an older audience (e.g., an oral presentation to the faculty). Each of these categories would be varied with the size of the audience, ranging from 0 to 100. The situations will be rank ordered and rated based on the level of discomfort produced. This will determine the most appropriate use of the VRT.

Reactions according to the **Subjective Units of Disturbance scale** will be collected every few minutes during exposure on a 0 (no discomfort) to 10 (panic-level anxiety) scale. This is a very quick and simple measure of anxiety. The method has been used widely and been shown to correlate well with objective physiological measures of anxiety (Thyer et al, 1984).

The instruments used in the pilot studies were of a self-reporting nature. The validity of the data depended on the attitude, honesty, and accuracy of the participants' responses. Current literature regarding virtual environments recommends the use of physiological data (e.g., heart rate, blood pressure, galvanic skin response, EEG/EMG, etc.) to measure the sense of presence. For instance, Barfield addresses this issue and writes that techniques which measure sense of presence typically and primarily involve subjective assessment, which is most useful for initial exploration and hypothesis generation (Barfield and Weghorst, 1993). Barfield's hypothesis is that as sense of presence increases within a virtual environment. The participant should experience physiological changes that can be measured and analyzed to determine the optimal sense of presence with a minimal visual presentation of virtual environment scenes and objects. Therefore the researchers would like to use physiometric indicators of sense of presence which are readily quantifiable. The physiological instruments will be used to measure various changes in subjects' bodily functions. The changes in bodily functions are indicators of physiological arousal purportedly linked to virtual reality sense of presence and performance.

Apparatus

Hardware for this study will consist of a Pentium based computer (100 MHZ or higher), head-mounted display (CyberEye,Virtual Reality Inc.), and an electromagnetic sensor that will be used to track the head (Flock of Birds, Ascension Technology) so that the user may interact with objects in the virtual world. Modeling will be done by using VREAM Virtual Reality Development Software Package and Libraries to create virtual reality scenes from the models representing a customized hierarchy of fear producing situations.

Virtual Reality Scene

A model of the auditorium located on the first floor of the CAU Research Science and Technology building will be created. The auditorium is 48 feet wide, 100 feet long and 55 feet high. The seating area has three sections of chairs and can accommodate over 100 people. A wooden podium with a speaker's stand are among the specific features of the facility. An amplifier with direct connection to the virtual reality software and hardware will be used in the therapy session. This will enable the subjects to hear their voices echo, simulating the echo of the real auditorium through a headphone attached to the head-mounted display.

Procedure

The treatment schedule will consist of eight weekly sessions for the ISD and VRT conditions. Session length will be 45 minutes for the first session and 15 minutes for each of the seven subsequent sessions. VRT will be conducted in the Virtual Reality Technology Laboratory on the Clark Atlanta University (CAU) campus. ISD will be conducted in the CAU Psychology Department. The control subjects will report for the treatment expectancy self-rating and the repeated assessment in the Psychology Department.

In the first treatment session, the ISD subjects will be asked to rank order a list of public speaking situations that induce fear, based on the degree of anxiety they arouse. These hierarchies will be used later for the ISD (Pendleton and Higgins, 1983). Subjects will meet as a group for 30 minutes of relaxation training. During the VRT subjects' first session, they will be familiarized, as a group, with the virtual reality equipment. At the conclusion of the session, they will receive 30 minutes of relaxation training as a group.

For the VRT and ISD subjects' subsequent sessions, individual systematic desensitization therapy will be conducted in a standard format. The computer program designed for VRT will generate a standard hierarchy of fearful public speaking situations to be presented at the same rate in VRT and ISD. Assessment measures will be administered under blind conditions and in a standard order. Therapists will have comparable training, professional backgrounds and training in behavioral therapy.

To assess the subjects, each of the three subject groups will be administered the Fear Questionnaire and the modified SUD at pretreatment, post-treatment and one month post-treatment. At the end of the fourth session, a nine-point rating scale to assess the therapist's support and subject motivation will be completed by the ISD and VRT subjects only. A nine-point rating scale to assess the expectancy of the treatment effectiveness will be completed by subjects in all three conditions.

At the one month post treatment, all subjects will be asked to complete a nine-point scale to rate the degree to which their fear symptoms have changed since the post-treatment test (Improved Rating Scale). After follow-up testing, all subjects will be encouraged to begin employing relaxation techniques when exposed to fearful situation. At the completion of all treatment of the ISD and VRT groups, the control group will be offered VRT treatment.

OBSESSIVE-COMPULSIVE DISORDERS

Approximately five million people just in United States, one in fifty Americans, suffer with obsessive-compulsive disorder (OCD) which affects their normal lives. For example, one might have an overwhelming urge to arrange a room's furniture, dishes in the cupboards, and books in shelves. Someone else will wash their hands repeatedly, regardless of how many times that day they had already done so. These compulsive behaviors definitely interfere with the every day activities of the patients and bring about disturbing thoughts that cause anxiety. Ironically, patients perform these repetitive behaviors to alleviate anxiety.

OCD can be found in men, women, and children of all races, and socioeconomic backgrounds. The most common obsessions include fear of contamination, fear of making mistakes, and fear of harm to another. Common compulsions include cleaning and washing, arranging and organizing, collecting, counting and repeating. Medication and behavior therapy are the most common treatments for OCD.

Since VRT appears to alleviate anxiety in patients with phobic disorders, it may also be useful in the treatment of OCD. For example, a scene can be created for a patient who compulsively rearranges books on the bookshelf until she sees that there is no point in continuing this behavior or basically becomes desensitized to it. Feelings of insecurity, shame, inadequacy, and powerlessness may not be as strong in the virtual scene as they are in the real world experience.

Most OCD patients not only are ashamed of their uncontrollable repetitive behavior but are very much concerned with what other people think of them when seeing their obsessive-compulsive behavior. At the very least, VRT has the potential to reduce the patient's embarrassment and provide privacy. In turn, it offers the patient a chance to concentrate on the problem, thereby reducing information overload and releasing cognitive resources to seek an alternative to the obsessive-compulsive behavior.

For example, an OCD patient can work on changing her inner dialogue (self-talk) while under the influence of VRT. She can experience no adverse consequences in the virtual world, which may help to reassure her. A patient who in real life habitually and repeatedly retraces her driving route to make sure that she has not run over an animal or person can rest assured that the virtual roads in her virtual scene do not contain any other living objects. She can also be instructed to reduce the number of times she repeats her obsessive-compulsive behavior. Or she can use the alternative approach and repeat her behavior as long as she wishes until she becomes desensitized. Also, when she feels the urge to repeat the compulsive behavior she can stop her virtual car whenever she wants to. That's not necessarily possible while driving on a busy highway in the real world; it would be too dangerous. In the virtual world, the patient can stop her car, and the other cars may also stop at her command. A patient who is obsessed with washing her hands repeatedly to avoid contamination can be assured that there is no contamination in the newly created virtual world that she is entering.

This will provide a scenario that makes no sense to her in terms of her normal thought processes. VRT scenarios of this kind will prompt a patient to become willing to take a risk and allow herself to experience new ways of thinking, feeling, and acting. Of course, we are eager to test these hypotheses and scenarios in the months ahead.

Besides the medication approach, there are several behavior therapy approaches in the treatment of OCD. In this section only a few common ones are briefly introduced to allow readers to understand the possible use of VRT to combat OCD. For detailed information about the nature of OCD and its treatment, see the book by Edna Foa and Reid Wilson, 1991, and the book by Edmund J. Bourne, 1995 which can be found in the reference section of this book.

- Accepting Obsessing—The patient is placed in a virtual scene and allowed to accept her OCD, repeating the compulsive behavior until it passes. With the magnified stimuli that VRT techniques produce, this could lead to simple desensitization, reducing or ending the patient's distress.
- Postponing Obsessing—The patient is asked to intentionally delay obsessing for a short period of time. At first she may delay it for a minute, gradually lengthening the delay to several minutes or an hour or more. This can be easily done under VRT conditions, allowing the patient to gain a sense of control over her OCD.
- Creative Distractions—Channelling the attention of the patient to an interesting distraction, such as reading a book or watching a favorite movie, have proven helpful in treating some OCD patients. Of course, the very condition of virtual presence within VRT also distracts the patient's thoughts from the real world and allows her to ignore her obsessive behavior and become desensitized.
- Experiencing the Worst—Continuous exposure to the worst-case scenario has been helpful in desensitizing OCD patients. The VRT is a safe environment in which the patient can repeatedly perform the worst-case acts of compulsion and obsession until desensitized.

The patient in a virtual reality scene can safely and comfortably allow herself a time for rest and relaxation. She can repeat activities at a different pace, under her control, which has been shown to be helpful with most patients suffering from anxiety.

We have began to conduct several pilot case studies to test the effectiveness of VRT in patients with OCD.

ATTENTION DEFICIT DISORDERS

Attention Deficit Disorder (ADD) is common among children. Current research indicates that between five and ten percent of children suffer from this disorder. Many of these children are highly intelligent and creative despite wandering attention and impulsiveness. Because they have problems with short term memory and short attention spans, they have a hard time completing tasks. They have trouble concentrating, being easily distracted, mostly by sights and sounds. They especially exhibit problems in a group situation (Hunsucker, 1993).

In general, the ADD patients' problems are physical, academic, behavioral, emotional, and social.

Traditional treatment for ADD includes medications such as Methylphenidate (Ritalin), D-Amphetamine (Dexedrine), and Pemoline (Cylert). Behavioral management also includes punishment and reward techniques.

Several research studies in this book have shown that virtual reality technology provides specific stimuli that can be used in removing distractions and providing environments that get the subjects' attention and increases their concentration. Virtual reality technology can hold a patient's attention for a longer period of time than other methods can. These scenes may enhance the patient's short term memory and increase attention span. Researchers at CAU's Virtual Reality Technology Laboratory are developing several classroom situation scenes to extensively test these hypotheses. As a matter of fact, an informal pilot study conducted in this lab showed that a patient's mild ADD symptoms decreased while under VRT. Although we have used only visual stimuli, the preliminary observations are very encouraging. There is good evidence from our previous research that this kind of experience may be easily transferred to everyday activities. The ongoing ADD research will be extended to include other stimuli such as auditory and tactile. A scenario for social interaction is also under development, to test the effects of VRT in teaching patients the interaction needed to improve their social skills.

POST-TRAUMATIC STRESS DISORDERS

During World War I, soldiers in combat were observed to suffer chronic anxiety, nightmare, and flashbacks that lasted for days and even years. Severe traumas such as war, earthquakes, tornadoes, car or plane crashes, assault and rape can produce intense fear, and feelings of helplessness. Disabling reactions to such traumatic events fall into the category of disorders known as post-traumatic stress disorder, or PTSD in short. PTSD causes a variety of symptoms, such as intense flashbacks, nightmares, and repetitive disturbing thoughts about the traumatic event. Other symptoms are feelings of detachment from others, being out of touch with one's own feelings, increased anxiety and, most importantly, avoidance of activities related to the trauma. Exposure therapy has been used to treat patients with PTSD, enabling them to work through the intense fear caused by the traumatic event (Shapiro, 1995).

There is a great deal of similarity between phobias (such as agoraphobia) and PTSD. However, PTSD is more intense. Just as VRT has been utilized to treat patients with various phobias, it may also be used to treat patient with PTSD. Virtual reality scenes can be created to match some of the salient cues provided by patients. Of course, based on our previous experience, it is not necessary to create a virtual world that exactly matches the real world events. Only a few important cues provided by the patient may be sufficient to recreate an experience in the patient's mind. A modification of our innovative VRT methodology for treating patients with agoraphobia may be useful in treating PTSD people, particularly if it can help them to reexperience the traumatic event in the safe environment of virtual reality. VRT makes it possible for a virtual therapist to accompany the patient while revisiting a traumatic scene. For example, a simplified scene of a Vietnam war zone is under development in our Laboratory. It mimics the dense jungle growth with plants and trees similar to what grows in the actual physical location. In this virtual jungle scene, we will allow our subjects a walk-through while the virtual therapist goes with them and assures them that it is a safe place. The virtual jungle scene with minimal cues may evoke the original traumatic memory and allow the patient to become desensitized. By repeating the virtual experience the fear would be gradually reduced. As mentioned in earlier sections, in VRT patients gain a sense of self-control, regain self-esteem and become willing to take some risks. In doing so, they permit themselves to grow. Eventually more intense cues may be introduced into the virtual scene, such as the sound of machine guns heard from a distance. This may evoke other related traumatic events, allowing the patient to become more desensitized.

THERAPEUTIC AUGMENTED REALITY

In traditional psychotherapy, the goal has been to change the patient to fit reality. A new branch of therapy seeks to change reality to fit the patient. An example of this came from Dr. Suzanne Weghorst, director of Interface Development, Human Interface Technology, at the University of Washington. She described an ongoing case study involving a patient suffering from Parkinson's disease. This patient is being treated by augmented reality technology. Dr. Weghorst, reporting on this case at the *Medicine Meets Virtual Reality IV Conference '96* in San Diego, argued that traditional psychotherapy has focused on modifying behavior by changing the client's internal processes, be they perceptions, interpretations, articulations, contingency associations, or deeper psychoanalytic processes. The goal of therapy, from these perspectives, is to change the client to better fit reality. Augmented reality, or the merging of artificial and natural stimuli, affords the possibility of modifying behavior by altering the client's sensory inputs, in essence changing reality to better fit the client. This approach may be quite effective for certain disorders, particularly those due to specific neurological dysfunction, and may provide an alternative to pharmacological treatment.

Dr. Weghorst anticipates at least two broad applications of augmented reality in psychotherapy: (1) as a tool to enhance face-to-face therapeutic techniques, and (2) as a "perceptual prosthesis" for everyday use by the client. An example of the former might be in directing the client's attention to the therapist or to some object of discourse. This application would benefit from a collaborative form of augmented reality which she has termed "shared space."

One fortuitous application of the second approach to augmented reality therapy has been demonstrated in the treatment of Parkinson's

Disease. Capitalizing on a well-known but little used visual cuing phenomenon (kinesia paradoxa), appropriate artificial cues can enable
akinetic patients to walk, reducing the severity of dyskinesia resulting
from long-term drug treatment. Ancillary positive effects on affect and
cognitive functioning have also been observed.

Augmented reality technology is currently in its infancy and its
practical applications are somewhat limited. In particular, current visual
display methods suffer from restricted field of view, relatively poor
spatial resolution, and insufficient brightness in competition with normal ambient light levels. Solutions to these technological problems are
in sight, however, and long-term prospects for augmented reality
therapy are intriguing.

INTERNET-MEDIATED VISUALIZATION IN BEHAVIOR THERAPY

Classical psychotherapy involves direct interaction between a therapist
and a patient or a group of patients, usually at the therapist's office.
Recently, therapists have been experimenting with conducting group
sessions in cyberspace. The therapist is in his home, and the clients are
in their homes, using personal computers. Employing what is known on
the Internet as a "chat room," this group therapy approach appears to
have been highly effective, although limited due to the lack of
visualization.

Dr. Hans Sieburg, a psychiatrist at the University of California at
Berkeley is investigating the effects of visual cues in psychotherapy
conducted via the Internet, using Virtual Reality Modeling Language
(VRML)—a unique approach. The product to be developed is the
prototype of a behavior modification server based on VRML visualiza-
tion ("Skinner Engine"). The San Diego Supercomputer Center and the
Laboratory for Biological Informatics & Theoretical Medicine at the
Departments of Psychiatry and Mathematics will collaborate on the
research. This clinical trial is to be conducted in the laboratory at
UCSD, and at a selected number of homes in the San Diego area.

When completed, the proposed visualization will become available
to a group of individuals partaking in a clinical trial of the VRML tool
in behavior therapy.

Dr. Sieburg's research group addresses three specific applications of increasing difficulty; he reports:

Internet-mediated Treatment of Acrophobia

Recently, a number of groups, most notably those of Ralph Lamson and Max North et al, have reported encouraging results in the treatment of acrophobia—the fear of heights. This work was conducted using single immersive environments. To properly develop our proposed technology, and to have data to which we can compare our observations, we propose to initially develop a VRML environment conducive to treating acrophobia over the Internet. This has several further advantages. For example, the environment does not yet require VRML "behaviors," and therefore clinical testing can proceed while VRML is developed further. Finally, we will be able to test remote biofeedback equipment developed at Loma Linda.

This project was completed in November 1995. The software can be licensed for use in clinical trials.

Internet-mediated Treatment of Social Phobias

Social phobias are common aversions to interactions with fellow humans. For example, the fear of constantly being evaluated affects a sizable population and prevents individuals from reaching their full potential. A VRML environment allows a subject to present a topic of her choice to an audience, or to answer questions in response to requests from that audience. The audience may be either a simulation of remote members of a therapy group or it may be a complete simulation. The most important difference between this and Project A is that VRML "behaviors" will be used in this scenario. These "behaviors" will allow for noise in the crowd, such as fidgeting, coughing and whispering. Such sounds may induce phobic responses in the patient. In some cases, crowd noise may be simulated by the supervising therapist to monitor very specific stimulus-response patterns. In other cases, a random behavior generator may be applied. Heads-up displays and biofeedback instruments will be applied as in the first project. This project is currently in progress.

Internet-mediated Visual Couples Therapy

The long-term aim of the study is to bring us full-circle with the results of textual group therapy. In particular, we will be able to apply the technology developed under the first and second projects to create an environment in which individual couples can describe themselves to a group of couples. In addition, there should be the possibility of inter-acting with a partner's VRML persona in order to describe behaviors deemed offensive or desirable. This approach seems to be promising in cases where it is difficult to achieve direct partner-to-partner communication in front of a therapist and other couples.

❖   ❖   ❖

The Future of VRT

Our innovative virtual reality therapy approach has created enormous excitement in the scientific community and has attracted a great deal of public attention. This excitement has led to the authorship of several conceptual papers for various audiences. Here we report on two such papers that we believe will provide a direction for the future of VRT. The first paper is written by a group of scientists from Massachusetts Institute of Technology. The complete report is in the journal of *Presence: Teleoperators and Virtual Environments*, Volume 5, No. 4, 1996. The second paper introduces the concept of using VRT as a "counseling center." Ms. Aretha Edling, a researcher at the University of North Texas explores this issue. These papers are partially reprinted here with the permission of the authors.

Virtual Reality And Psychotherapy: Opportunities and Challenges

Kalman Glantz, Ph.D., Nathaniel I. Durlach, Ph.D., Rosalind C. Barnett, Ph.D., Walter A. Aviles, M.S.D.
MIT Virtual Environment and Teleoperator Research Consortium (VETREC) and Virtual Reality Therapy, Inc.

Virtual reality technology is now being used to provide exposure and desensitization for a limited number of phobic conditions. The most obvious immediate candidates for VRT are other specific phobias, including fear of public speaking, fear of animals (such as snakes, spiders or rats), fear of medical procedures (e.g., blood or injections), and fear of the natural environment (storms, water, etc.). These conditions are generally treated with the same techniques as those used for acrophobia, agoraphobia, and fear of flying. For all these conditions, virtual reality probably has a high potential for convenience, realism, and matching to specific client needs. For example, one could create a snake that was unrealistically charming. It remains to be seen whether such modifications of the basic behavioral routines will produce superior results.

TOWARD THE FUTURE

It seems likely to us that virtual reality will eventually become far more than a tool to provide exposure and desensitization. Indeed, virtual reality technology may eventually create enough new capabilities to profoundly influence the shape of therapy. Several such potential capabilities are discussed in subsections below. In the last subsection we comment briefly on the feasibility of achieving some of the capabilities discussed.

Enhancement of Memory and Imagination

In the most general sense, the potential of virtual reality derives from the central role played, in both life and psychotherapy, by memory, imagination and anticipation. Almost everything humans do involves remembering and/or projecting forward. But memory and imagination have limits. Virtual reality can help to transcend those limits.

With virtual reality, one will eventually be able to recreate the past and create alternative futures. This will be done by "immersing" the client in an experience—a multi-modal virtual environment—that is more vivid and "real" than the worlds most people can summon with their memory or their imagination. What is so unique about the virtual reality environment is its interactivity. The user of virtual reality will learn by doing—speaking, moving, responding, initiating. Even though acts in the virtual world will not have the consequences of real acts, they will impact the virtual environment. Thus, the user of virtual reality will be a doer, and doing has a more powerful effect than passive participation.

Simulation of the Social Environment

It is probable that the ultimate potential of virtual reality for therapy lies in the simulation of the social, as opposed to the physical, environment. Creating effective simulations of human interactions is far more complicated than creating simulations of inanimate surroundings and goes far beyond the current capabilities of virtual reality technology. Still, it may become possible, and the more therapists develop a demand for it, the greater the probability that scientists will develop the required technology.

The ultimate challenge will be to create and animate virtual personae-characters who look, sound and "behave" like people who are significant in the client's life and memory (e.g., family members, friends, enemies, colleagues, and bosses). Ideally, it will become possible to create virtual personae (VPs) that resemble these significant others in general appearance, facial expression, voice quality, body language, and higher-level behavioral characteristics. Presumably such simulations would make use not only of physical media such as photographs and audio/video tapes, but also of computational models of behavior.

Client and therapist would be able to use such VPs for many purposes—to relive significant events, to say things that weren't said at the time, to experience a desired outcome, to otherwise provide closure on troublesome memories, to rehearse behaviors and social interactions.

VPs, often referred to as "agents," come in two types, guided and autonomous. As the level of technological difficulty is different for these two kinds of agents, we will discuss them separately.

An agent is guided when it is under complete control of an operator. We envisage that guided VPs controlled by the therapist will be used to respond to and interact with clients. For example, in a role-play, a therapist could speak through a guided VP tailored to represent the client's father or mother. Similarly, a client might use a guided VP that looks like her boss to role-play the boss's actions.

An agent is autonomous when its behavior is controlled by software programs (algorithms) that have been built into the virtual reality system. An autonomous VP could, for example, have a repertoire of behaviors developed in accordance with the client's memory of the behavior patterns of the individual in question. It could also have a set of behaviors that the client wishes the individual had evidenced. With this repertoire, it could respond differentially to the client depending on the client's behavior. It could also initiate certain behaviors on its own.

Creating effective VPs, especially autonomous ones, will be difficult. However, research and development is actively proceeding. Some of the most advanced work on autonomous VPs is being conducted at the Carnegie Mellon University's Computer Sciences Department. Researchers there have been trying to develop human-like agents that can be used to create works of fiction whose characters interact with the user in apparently spontaneous, creative ways. While the Carnegie Mellon group is still far from achieving this goal, researchers have developed agents with a gift for seemingly purposeful actions and interactions. The project, code-named Oz, has also identified four crucial characteristics for believable agents. First, the agent must freely react to user interventions, the actions of other agents, and changes in the environment. Second, the agent must be goal-directed. Third, the agent must display definite personality traits. Fourth, the agent must show appropriate emotions when engaging in activities. These characteristics are probably identical to those that will be needed for the effective use of VPs in psychotherapy (Sweeney, 1995).

Provisions of New Kinds of Experiences

The virtual world can provide experiences that are impossible in the real world. Some real-world experiences are simply too dangerous or too threatening to try in therapy. Other types of experience are simply impossible; one can't rearrange life the way one can organize a simulation. Forays into the virtual world can enable clients to master new skills, experiment with new roles, and thereby develop the creativity necessary to overcome maladaptive habits, thoughts and emotions.

Participation of the Therapist

Therapists will actually be able to participate with the client in the simulated environments, both past and future. They will be able to experience the same stimuli and observe the client's reaction in real time, rather than inferring information from verbal reports. This possibility holds enormous promise. We have already discussed how virtual reality makes it possible for the therapist to participate, at relatively low-cost, in vivo desensitization. In the future, a virtual reality therapist might, for example, be a supportive presence as a client role-plays a difficult interview or grapples with an unfamiliar social situation. Similarly, a therapist might accompany a client on a memory tour of an abusive childhood. In each case, the therapist could provide the same kind of support and guidance that the client would be given in the real world.Ultimately, the virtual world will allow therapists to "accompany" their clients in a vastly expanded set of situations, opening up the possibility of new and different types of shared experience, the nature of which cannot now be foreseen.

Touch

Virtual reality technology will offer unique opportunities to treat disorders in which touching is an important issue (e.g., fear of intimacy). Touching is an extremely powerful form of social interaction. Nevertheless, in most forms of therapy, touching is strongly discouraged for a variety of reasons: boundary violations, the possibility of abuse, and the need for therapists to protect themselves against accusations of improper behavior. Virtual reality will make it possible for the therapist to design experiences that include "virtual touching." For example, a virtual person guided by the therapist could grasp the hand of a virtual person guided by the client. This would add an entirely new dimension to psychotherapy.

On Feasibility

It is obvious that the above-mentioned capabilities will take some time to develop. However, the difficulties may not be as great as they seem. One should not assume, for example, that virtual reality needs to be totally realistic to be effective. A given stimulus can often be vastly simplified without seriously altering the response to that stimulus. This is the basis of the notion of "effective stimulus" in psychology. Thus it seems likely that simplified social situations will be adequate to produce therapeutic results. In other words, even highly simplified scenes drawn from a client's personal memory, wish list, nightmare, or catastrophic expectation, will be of therapeutic use. If this proves to be the case, then the capabilities described above, and in particular the development of effective VPs, may not be as difficult as it now seems.

THE NEXT GENERATION OF APPLICATIONS

The first applications of these new capabilities will probably be concerned with conditions that, although more complex than simple phobias, still involve anxiety as the key symptom. We briefly discuss three such conditions.

Social Phobia (a.k.a. Rejection Sensitivity)

Social phobia, a complex and common condition in which people withdraw from social contact because it is so painful, is now being treated with some success with anti-depressants, including selective serotonin reuptake inhibitors (SSRI's) such as Prozac and Zoloft, and monoamine oxidase inhibitors (MAOI's) such as Nardil. However, these medications have significant side-effects, especially sexual, so anything that could replace the medication, or even lower the dose necessary to produce a therapeutic effect, would be welcome. Besides, behavior therapy is frequently used in addition to medication. Hence the need for better behavioral treatments.

According to John Marshall, author of Social Phobia (1994), people suffering from this condition often have what amounts to sub-phobias. At least two of these, "bashful bladder" (inability to urinate in public) and fear of eating in public, are in essence simple phobias that could be treated with the same approach now being used for other simple phobias.Eliminating one or several sub-phobias might have a substantial impact on the social phobias.

Tackling the social phobia itself would be more complicated. In conventional therapy, exposure to the kinds of situations feared by social phobias often involves role-playing, with the therapist playing opposite the client (Marshall, 1994). One of the limitations of conventional role-playing is the "unreality" of it. The therapist is NOT the feared figure, and therefore the role-play may not necessarily evoke sufficient anxiety. In addition, the client often feels that "pretending" is silly. An advanced virtual reality would be well-suited to overcome these limitations, because role-playing with virtual reality could be far more immersive and realistic, provided effective VPs can be developed.

Fear of Intimacy

Fear of intimacy is generally treated with psychotherapy rather than behavior therapy. Even though exposure is desirable, how does one provide exposure to "intimacy?" The use of surrogates has been tried and rejected. Opposite-sex surrogates encouraged intimacy and reinforced certain aspects of the client's behavior. However, the potential for unanticipated negative consequences was too high and this intervention has been abandoned. The answer to the above question that has proved most satisfactory has been: through the relationship with the therapist.

The therapeutic relationship will undoubtedly remain crucial to the treatment of fear of intimacy, but virtual reality technology could prove to be a useful adjunct. The idea would be to create a VP, guided or autonomous, with which the client could interact in an intimate manner. The VP might have the features and character of someone the client was currently trying to be, or wanted to be, intimate with. To what extent the effectiveness of such an intervention will depend on the fidelity/ accuracy of the simulation is an important area of research.

Intimacy is a difficult and somewhat nebulous concept, but it can be perhaps be broken down into such components as proximity, touch, tone of voice, etc. Discovering the constituent components of intimacy is an interesting area of research, perhaps akin to ethological work on the components of animal communication.

Despite the difficulties inherent in generating such simulations, the effort might be worthwhile. Fear of intimacy is widespread and is frequently found in trauma victims. Conventional psychotherapy for these individuals is long and costly.

Sexual Aversion

Some people have a persistent or recurrent phobic reaction to sexual activity. The ability of virtual reality to simulate proximity and touch, and to generate realistic interactions with a VPs, without incurring the risk of sexual abuse, real or imagined, makes virtual reality an especially promising technology for this condition. We realize, of course, that there are ethical and perhaps legal ramifications that would need to be considered before the technology could be applied in this manner.

POSSIBLE FUTURE USES OF VIRTUAL REALITY IN THERAPY

In the following subsections, we outline a few of the possible interventions that may ultimately be enhanced by virtual reality technology. We realize fully that some of what we described may never come to pass and some may prove not to be useful. But new horizons call for freedom of the imagination, not the security of established doctrines.

Exploration of Childhood Memories

In the earlier section, we mentioned that virtual reality could be used to enhance memory and imagination. How might a therapist whose stock in trade is the exploration of childhood memories (i.e., exploratory therapy) use virtual reality in psychotherapy?

Therapists use a variety of interventions to facilitate exploration. Clients are asked to express buried emotions, to engage in dialogues with an imaginary parent, to say things that they wished they had said, to exchange places with significant others, to imagine how they would have liked to be treated, etc. With virtual reality, one might create virtual parents, siblings and other significant figures with whom the clients could interact, thus bringing to vivid life important scenes from the past. The things that need to be said would be said to a realistic VP instead of, for example, to an empty chair, as in gestalt therapy. Emotions such as anger and grief would be expressed directly to the virtual representation of the person the client wanted as a witness, instead of to the therapist. The words the client wants to hear would come from a VP who looks and sounds like the person the client wanted those words to come from. Role reversals, another standard technique, would be startlingly realistic. In this sense, virtual reality would make it possible to animate the unconscious. The realism and multi-sensorial nature of such re-creations should greatly enhance the healing power of these interventions. Note also that, as we pointed out earlier, the therapist can be brought onto the scene to act as guide and supporting presence.

Enhancing Cognitive Therapy

Maladaptive thinking is the major focus of cognitive therapy. In the following remarks, we focus on two related aspects of maladaptive thinking: incorrect assumptions and incorrect interpretations. We use the former term to denote stable concepts about the nature of the world. Some examples are: "A knight on a white horse will some day carry me away," and "Everything I do is doomed to failure." We use the term "interpretation" to denote ad hoc concepts about immediate situations (e.g., "That must mean he doesn't like me."). There is of course considerable overlap: "interpretations" often depend on "assumptions." Nevertheless the distinction is useful in many therapeutic situations.

Everyone makes assumptions about the nature of the world and these assumptions are often deeply rooted in personal history. When the assumptions are self-defeating, they need to be changed. Cognitively-oriented therapists challenge assumptions in a variety of ways: they reason; they ask for evidence in favor of the assumption, hoping to expose its fallacious roots; they may try to uncover the origins of the assumption, the better to refute it; they identify the emotions that are associated with the maladaptive thinking; and so on. Nevertheless, people often have a hard time giving up their assumptions, no matter how self-defeating.

One reason it is so difficult to get people to update their assumptions is that change often requires a prior step—recognizing the distinction between an assumption and a perception. Until revealed to be fallacious, assumptions constitute the world; they seem like perceptions, and as long as they do, they are resistant to change.

We anticipate using virtual reality to help people in distress make the distinction between assumptions and perceptions. It is of interest that virtual reality's capacity to do this has already been noted in the scientific community:

"The perceptual world created by out senses and nervous system is so functional a representation of the physical world that most people live out their lives without ever suspecting that contact with the physical world is mediate... Oddly enough, the newly developing technology of... virtual displays is having the unexpected effect of promoting such insight, for the impression of being in the ... simulated environment experienced by the user.... can be so compelling as to force a user to question the assumption that the physical and perceptual worlds are one and the same" (Loomis, 1992).

In simpler language, virtual reality is a highly advanced system for creating illusory worlds—realities that fool the senses. With virtual reality, one can actually demonstrate that what looks like a perception doesn't really exist. This gets across the idea that a person can have a false perception. Once this has been understood, individual maladaptive assumptions can then be challenged more easily.

The same process should help with maladaptive interpretations. Everyone has to "interpret" ambiguous situations and most situations are ambiguous to some degree. Problems arise when an individual's interpretations stray too far from consensual reality.Cognitive therapists tend to deal with interpretations much as they deal with assumptions, i.e., they use a mixture of support and reason.

There are at least two ways one might use virtual reality in this area. First, one could simulate situations directly related to the problematic interpretations. The therapist could recreate scenes and employ VPs that are capable of interacting with the client. Clients could then test their interpretations against the (virtual) reality. This reality could be shaped to bring about the desired learning. Second, one could create environments that are both very convincing (immersive) and highly ambiguous—the virtual reality equivalent of optical illusions. By constructing scenarios that, like the Necker cube or the Boring figure, can be easily interpreted in at least two dramatically opposing fashions, it should be possible to enhance a client's appreciation of ambiguity and hence the active role of assumptions and perceptions in the act of interpreting external events.

A procedure related to these ideas is already available in the TAT (Thematic Apperception Test), a set of cards depicting ambiguous scenes that clients are asked to interpret. But instead of using the figures and scenes as a testing device, one could use virtual reality to demonstrate to the client the active role of the brain in producing an interpretation of the scene. Once this understanding had been established, one could proceed, perhaps without virtual reality, to analyze and correct the client's specific interpretations.

Increasing Freedom and Expanding Options

A variety of factors conspire to limit the options people think are available to them. We discuss two of these factors below.

Stimulus-dependence

Some people go through life feeling compelled to respond to what other people do. They experience each impulse and/or emotion as a reaction —a response to something someone else has done or to something that has happened. Thus, they believe that they have no choices; they "can't help themselves." In the jargon of therapy, they place the locus of control outside of themselves.

People with this problem often have strong feelings that they attribute to others—they believe that other people are the cause of those feelings. In such cases, the compulsion to respond is aggravated by the strength of the emotions. In other words, the feelings function as motivational states requiring action. People with this problem don't have the option of not responding or of responding differently to a stimulus.

Conventional therapy seeks, of course, to "empower" such people. One way to do so is by helping them to experience an impulse or emotion as a physiological process separate from the external stimulus. When the response becomes independent of the stimulus, the individual has more autonomy, more freedom of action, and can recognize more options.

Virtual reality might be able to make a special contribution to the treatment of this problem. In virtual reality, the external situation/stimulus does not really exist. The "unreality" of the virtual reality stimulus can be used to help clients grasp the idea that their internal states (thought or feeling) can be independent of the external stimulus. Once this "meta-learning" has been achieved, the client should be in a better position to recognize the separation of stimulus and response in many different situations.

Grasping the independence of response from stimulus shifts locus of control; clients can learn to actively operate on their environments rather than passively submit/react to events beyond their control. They can focus on changing their own reactions instead of fatalistically believing that they would have to change the world to improve their situation.

Learned helplessness

Many people go through life with a feeling of helplessness. They don't believe they have any effect on other people or any ability to control their own destiny.

Conventional therapy seeks to empower such people by providing support and encouragement, by helping them develop and rehearse new strategies, and by helping them overcome their fear of taking risks.

All of these interventions can be enhanced by giving these clients the power to create their own "realities" —to play God in the virtual environment.Clients could create and operate VPs, purely as an exercise in power, or they could develop a life scenario and make it come out any way they wanted. By experiencing great power in the virtual world, they could learn to have some power in the real world.

One thing this might do is uncover hidden impulses and desires. For example, helplessness sometimes serves as a mask for aggression, anger and hatred. Once uncovered, such impulses would become available to be worked through in conventional therapy. (This application requires that the virtual reality apparatus be simple enough to allow people without much training to create situations and change outcomes. Much development will be needed to make this possible.)

Another way of approaching the problem of helplessness would be to encourage playfulness in the virtual environment. There are several connections between play and power. If you don't think you have any power, you can't play. If you think something vitally important is at stake and the outcome depends on your making just the right move, you can't play; it's too serious. In a simulated environment, one can play without fear, and so learn about the possibilities of play in the real world. In this connection, it's interesting to note that a Japanese team has already created a virtual sand box for use with disturbed children (Kijima et al., 1994).

Increasing Empathy

Many people have trouble understanding other people's points of view. Conventional therapy often employs role-playing to overcome this limitation, but as we mentioned in the discussion of social phobia, conventional role-play has significant limits; it often seems unreal and silly. The use of VPs could overcome this limitation. Client and therapist could each control a VP that had been created using photographs, video and audiotapes, as well as appropriate behavioral models. They could then exchange roles to promote the ability to see both sides of a situation. Note that the use of virtual reality to increase empathy across social classes, ethnic groups, and even across species has already been explored in the context of elementary education (Moshell and Hughes, 1994).

Developing and Solidifying Boundaries

The notion of "personal boundaries," though quite difficult to define and talk about, is often a major focus of psychotherapy. It is possible that virtual reality could provide some new ways to help people develop a stronger sense of personal boundaries. One way would be perceptual: experiment with manipulating (expanding or contracting)the boundaries of two VPs, a representation of self and a representation of another. Simulated touch could play a role here. Another way would be interactional: use VPs to role-play relationships involving over-involvement, under-involvement and excessive reactivity. At the least, such simulations should make it easier to talk about the issue.

It is important to mention here the view expressed by some people that using virtual reality could actually blur boundaries. Two concerns have been raised: (1) that excessive use of virtual reality could cause people to become so immersed in the virtual world that they withdraw from the real world (as apparently happened to a few fanatic players of Dungeons and Dragons); and (2) that some people's grip on reality is so fragile that exposure to a virtual world could cause them serious difficulty. These are important issues; proper screening, preparation, and monitoring will be essential.

Learning to Express Emotions

Many people are afraid to express their emotions. They fear retaliation if they express anger, rejection if they express friendship or love, indifference if they express a desire. In conventional therapies, clients are encouraged to express their emotions in a variety of ways. For example, (1) clients express themselves to the therapist standing in for someone else; (2) clients smash an object such as a tennis racquet onto a surface such as a pillow; and (3) clients address an empty chair (gestalt therapy). In general, these techniques have the same limitations as other forms of role-play.

With virtual reality, emotions could be expressed to a VP standing in for the person the client needs to address. The VP could be programmed in such a manner as to respond with maximum therapeutic impact. Furthermore, the client could conceivably interact physically with the VP, using a haptic interface (one that facilities manual sensing and manipulation of virtual objects). This could elicit more intense and more focused emotion than conventional techniques.

In addition, virtual reality may provide clients with new ways to convey their perceptions, feelings, and ideas to their therapist. Even for highly verbal clients who are used to communicating successfully by means of spoken language, the availability of other media may prove useful. For clients with more limited verbal skills, the availability of such media could make a major difference.

Promoting Marital Satisfaction and Bonding

Various social psychology experiments have shown that assigning groups of people tasks that require collaboration tends to create bonds between them. Tasks involving shared danger are particularly effective in this respect. Shared danger is impossible to assign in conventional therapy, but simulating danger should be feasible with virtual reality.

We also anticipate using role reversal to improve martial relationships, perhaps by having each spouse control a VP representing the other spouse. Walking a few miles in the other's shoes should help some troubled couples extricate themselves from the bondage of incomprehension and anger.

Application of Virtual Reality to Counseling Methods

Aretha Edling, M.A.D.
University of North Texas

ABSTRACT

This paper defines and describes virtual reality and possible future applications in counseling methods and in behavior modification practices.

INTRODUCTION AND REVIEW OF LITERATURE

The information age has an impact on what people must know, how they interact with one another, as well as on how they do their work. With this in mind, the administration of Technology Trends Counseling Center (TTCC) believes that there is a need to redefine and redirect counseling methods and models to better equip its clients and to prepare them for life in this new age. With this vision TTCC is embarking upon research into incorporating instructional interactive software and virtual reality into current counseling programs.

Virtual Reality Counseling Attributes

The attributes of the chosen technology must be considered in order to identify matches between that technology and its support of counseling methods. In other words, what does the technology have that will help the counseling situations? Virtual reality systems' main attributes are:

- The clients would be able to explore existing places and things to which they would not normally have access. There are almost endless possibilities in the creation of virtual, or artificial worlds.
- The clients could explore real things that could not otherwise be examined without alterations of scale or size and time.
- The clients could create places and things with altered quantities. The client is connected to the virtual world, thus providing a feeling of presence.
- The clients would be able to control and interact with objects and people within the virtual world in non-realistic ways.
- The clients would be able to receive physical feedback provided by objects and people within this world (Pantelidis, 1993).

Any kind of world, including unreal worlds can be presented by virtual reality. In real life, one does not have much choice but to live with what one has available. However, a virtual world can be created in any way desired. This can be a very useful counseling device in that it causes the invisible to become visible. Robert Heinich, in *Instructional*

Media and the New Technologies of Instruction, says "The high-resolution moving images opens up exciting possibilities for dealing with interpersonal skills. The development of skills in interpreting and reacting to the behavior of other humans, which otherwise would require role-play or real-life interaction, can now be provided as an individual , self-paced simulation exercise" (Heinich, et al, 1993)

There is no way means that the counselor s or therapists would not be needed, it only means that their roles would be redefined. These therapists would have to be a very good managers and organizers, and would have to avoid the temptation to let the counseling center replace himself or herself. The exact nature and order of counseling activities within the center may be strictly controlled by the therapist or may be left in whole or in part up to the client. In most cases it would be advisable to control activities at the onset and gradually increase the client's freedom to choose activities as they demonstrate ability to assume responsibility for self-direction.

Feeling of Presence

People have a feeling of presence with virtual reality. They believe they are really "there." Everyone has had some feeling of presence by reading some emotionally or mentally stimulating book, or watching a movie. But with virtual reality, the objects in the environment are presented in three-dimensional images. This enables them to help a person visualize an event. The sound is 360 degrees—or all around the user—and body tracking helps support the illusion of presence. This body tracking allows the system to gauge where the he or she is in the world. It also, in the most realistically way possible, supports the presentation of images and sounds.

Interaction and Control

In counseling situations, it would be often desirable for the virtual world to mimic the real world. Users can pick up and move objects, open doors, walk around corners and exercise control over parts of the virtual environment. Here cause and effect can often be viewed more advantageous than it can be in the real world. Perhaps the client is estranged from a person, or a person is no longer living, and the client has unresolved issues with that person. With virtual reality, through simulations, it would be possible to bring them together, so they can see and touch each other, in a mutual environment even if in reality they are separated by long distances, or by death.

Feedback

Tactile and force feedback from objects and people support the illusion of presence. This is an important attribute of the technology for counseling.

SCENARIO

The "counseling center" does not look like the traditional counseling center. It might possibly even be the client's own home. There is neither receptionist nor counselors in view, but they are there within reach. Their roles are not less, only different as they guided their clients through the world of virtual reality. Instead there are computer terminals equipped with various simulation, role-playing and virtual reality software.Various counseling models have been modified into workbook interactive video form, and applications of virtual reality have been developed for many therapies. Rational Behavior Therapy, group role-playing, metacommunication therapy (searching for the underlying rules governing interaction), interactive therapy, group counseling therapy, imagery, and many other types of therapy—even psychotherapy—can be "tuned" into in an instant, simply by turning on the computer.

The center makes many uses of simulations—artificial reality, cyberspace, and telepresence. These simulations also embody telerobotics (controlling a robot from a distance) and telecollaboration (linking participants across distances).

Small children have a room of their own in this center. Here they can do play therapy or interact in virtual reality situations that would allow them to explain the intricacies of themselves and their environments that they don't understand. There is a counselor here also, but again, behind the scenes or in minimal interaction with the children. Those who have access to a computer might tune into a counselor on-line from their own home where they possibly feel more comfortable.

Older children and teenagers as well as adults are eager to be involved. They interact with others, same age, younger or older in group-like settings on-line and remain "unseen" or "anonymous." Or they might be watching an appropriate, animated scene that requires emotional, mental or social interaction. The user becomes a part of, and participates in, the scene, discusses the problem, and finally settles on a solution. All age groups are able to get to "scary" places by being allowed to observe, sense and manipulate objects and persons from a safe distance. The telepresence is also invaluable here because it allows the clients to participate actively which body movements in simulated situations. When using such a system the clients almost believe that they are actually at the site of the activity, but understanding that they are not. The telecollaboration involves linking of virtual reality work stations at different locations, so the clients can create shared visual environments.

The "counseling center" has become an important part of these clients lives. Here, they feel and experience a freedom of ideas and interactions that would not be possible in any other counseling situations. The potential for spiritual, emotional, mental and physical growth, health and healing are phenomenal.

RELATING COUNSELING TO ATTRIBUTES OF VIRTUAL REALITY

Counseling Situation 1
The Counseling Program

Perhaps the most important attribute at this time is the extent to which an environment can meet a client's needs. An application of virtual reality to counseling is to create an unnatural world in which its easier to do something, and then progressively make it more difficult, more natural and more realistic. This has previously been applied to physical and cognitive skills in the educational setting, but it could also be applied to emotional skills. Motivation is strongly enhanced if the designers incorporate elements that simulate fantasy, challenge, and curiosity, to real situation. But the real situation may be very dangerous, or might require a "apprentice training" can be modified and adapted (Lanier, 1992).

"Scaffolding" is often used in apprentice training. It is a form of training help. It is constructed with the use in apprentice training. It is form of training help. It is constructed with the use of a trainer, reference manuals or a mentor, as the beginner starts to learn new tasks. The scaffolding is removed, a little at a time, as the learner becomes more familiar with the requirements of the tasks involved. This training would be especially useful for persons with phobias. All the scaffolding is removed when the learner had mastered his skills, subsequently leaving the learner doing his tasks on his own.

For example, for a client who has difficulty coping with complexity in a certain situation, it is possible to start with a simple virtual world and make it more complex over time. In a counseling situation, the scaffolding might be a group, a counselor or therapist, or many years of financially expensive psychotherapy or other emotionally, physically or mentally expensive add-ons that cannot be changed. Through virtual reality, the real environment can be modified to eliminate the need for the add-ons. Simple replicas of the real environments, in which most of the complexities and distractions have been removed can be constructed. As the client becomes more familiar with how his environment became dysfunctional, and is ready to move ahead, intricacies and complications can be gradually added until finally the virtual world is very similar to the real world. Through this the scaffolding has been taken away and replaced with a world that is manageable because the client now understands and can proceed with making changes as may be necessary. Perhaps years of psychotherapy have just been eliminated through this process.

Counseling Situation 2
Visualization and Regression Therapy

Allowing the client to visualize what cannot be seen in the real world is another aspect of virtual reality. Understanding underlying reasons for learning and performing certain tasks is difficult for many people.

Abstract situations are clarified by being able to visualize a process to make it more comprehensible. Perhaps a client needs to understand the behavior of another person. In a virtual environment that client can explore reasons why that person's behavior is as it is by visualizing possible aspects of that behavior that could not be seen in the real world.

With regression therapy (a counselor mentally guiding a client back in time to when a trauma occurred), virtual reality would be invaluable in that childhood environments could be simulated. The counselor would facilitate the regression, keeping in mind that people learn things in relation to their environment, and these virtual situations prompt retention and recall. If an individual goes into a place that he or she has not been for a long time, memories flood back and the whole context of the earlier experience return (Lanier, 1992). The counselor would then guide the client through the complex situation to a level of greater health and wholeness.

Counseling Situation 3
Group Interaction

Two or more people can be connected together through virtual reality telepresence and telecollaborations systems. A number of people can be inside the same virtual space and can interact in the same simulated system (Dede, 1992). They can see each other and each of them is able to make changes in the internal environment that will affect all the others in the group. This is a great way to role play in that each person takes on the personal appearance of any participant the client chooses them to be. These will not be fully realistic, of course. Although the participants will look "computer," they will be able to retain their individual body movements, even though their physical appearance has been altered. Individual body movements are as individual as tones of voice, or someone's facial features. In the virtual environment everyone recognizes the body movements of others, but in real environments, people are less aware of them (Lanier, 1992).

Counseling Situation 4
On-line to Counselor or Therapist

Clients who have home computers could use modems for counseling homework, electronic mail, and database access. The state of Indiana educational system has implemented an impressive program called the Buddy System through which they have the ultimate goal of providing a computer for every elementary school student's home. This same concept could be applied to counseling centers for those clients who are more independent. An assessment of the Indiana system esteem and greater pride in their work." (Sawyer, 1992). This method could also deliver counseling to homebound clients. Because of age, physical disabilities, illness, or bad weather, many clients would benefit from being able to participate in counseling sessions via one-way video tele-conferencing using the computer facility as the teleconferencing interface.

References

Abelson, J.L.,and Curtis, G.C. (1989).Cardiac and neuroendocrine responses to exposure therapy in height phobics. *Behaviour Research and Therapy 27*, 561-567.

Adame, D. D., Radell, S.A., Johnson, T.C., and Cole S.P. (1991). Physical fitness, body Image, and locus of control in college women dancers and nondancers. *Perceptual and Motor Skills, 72*, 91-95.

Agresti, A. (1990). *Categorical data analysis.* New York: John Wiley and Sons.

Allamani, A., and Allegranzi, P. (1990). Immagine corporea: Dimensioni e misure. Una ricerca clinica (Body Image: Dimensions and measures. A clinic research.). *Archivio di Psicologia Neurologia Psichiatria, 2*, 171-195.

American Psychiatric Association (1994). *Diagnostic and statistical manual of mental disorders (4th ed.).* Washington, D. C.

American Psychiatric Association (1980). *Diagnostic and statistical manual of mental disorders (3rd ed.).* Washington, D. C.

Ary, D., Jacobs, L.C., and Razavich A. (1983). *Introduction to research in education.* New York: Holt, Rinehart and Winston.

Ayres, J., and Hopf, T.S. (1985). A means of reducing speech anxiety. *Communication Education, 34*, 318-323.

Baars, B.J. (1988). *A cognitive theory of consciousness.* New York: Cambridge University Press.

Bajura, M. Fuchs, H., and Ohbuchi, R. (1992). Merging virtual objects with the real world: Seeing ultrasound imagery within the patient. *Computer Graphics, 26*(2), 203-210.

Bandura, A. (1977). *Social learning theory.* Englewood Cliffs, NJ: Prentice-Hall.

Barfield, W., and Weghorst, S. (1993). The sense of presence within virtual Environments: A conceptual framework. In G. Salvendy and M. J. Smith (Eds.) *Human-Computer Interaction: Software and Hardware Interfaces.* New York: Elsevier Science Publishers.

Barham, P.T., and McAllister, D.F. (1991). A comparison of stereoscopic cursors for the interactive manipulation of B-splines. *Proceedings of Stereoscopic Display and Applications II*, 18-26.

Barrios, B.A., Ruff, G., and York, C. (1989). Bulimia and body image: Assessment and explication of a promising construct. In W.G. Johnson (Ed.), *Advances in Eating Disorders Vol. II*. New York: Jay Press.

Belkin, G.S. (1988). *Introduction to counseling*. Dubuque: Wm. C. Brown Publishing.

Benedikt, M. (Ed.), (1991). *Cyberspace: First steps*. Cambridge, MA: MIT Press.

Bennett, K.B., Toms, M.L., and Woods, D.D. (1993). Emergent features and graphical elements: Designing more effective configural displays. *Human Factors, 35*(1), 71-97.

Boldovici, J. (1993). *Simulator Motion*. (ARI Technical Report No. 961) Alexanddria, VA: U.S. Army Research Institute for the Behavioral and Social Sciences.

Bourne, E.J., (1995). *The anxiety & phobia workbook (2nd ed.)*. Oakland, CA: New Harbinger Publications.

Bower, G.H. (1981). Mood and memory. *American Psychologist, 36,* 129-148.

Bricken, M, and Byrne, C. (1993). Summer students in virtual reality: A pilot study on educational applications in virtual reality technology. In Wexelblat, A.(Ed). *Virtual Reality Applications and Explorations* (pp. 199-217). Toronto: Academic Press Professional.

Bruch, H. (1962). Perceptual and conceptual disturbances in anorexia nervosa. *Psychosomatic Medicine, 24,* 187-194.

Bruch, H. (1973). *Eating disorders: Obesity, anorexia nervosa and the person within*. New York: Basic Books.

Bryson, S. (1992). Survey of Virtual Environment Technologies and Techniques. Computer Science Corporation, Applied Research Branch, Numerical Aerodynamic Simulation Systems Division, MST045-1, NASA Ames Research Center, *ACM SIGGRAPH '92 Course Notes*.

Burdea, G., and Coiffet, P. (1994). *Virtual reality technology*. New York: John Wiley & Sons.

Butters, J.W., and Cash, T.F. (1987). Cognitive-behavioral treatment of women's body image satisfaction: A controlled outcome-study. *Journal of Consulting and Clinical Psychology, 55,* 889-897.

Button, E. (1986). Body size perception and response to in-patient treatment in anorexia nervosa. *International Journal of Eating Disorders, 5,* 617-629.

Campos, J.J., Bertenthal, B.I., and Kermoian, R. (1992). Early experience and emotional development: The emergence of wariness of heights. *Psychological Science, 3,* 61-64.

Carroll, J.M. and Mack, R.L. (1985). Metaphor, computing systems, and active learning. *International Journal of Man-Machine Studies, 22,* 39-57.

Casper, R.C., Halmi, K., Goldberg, S.C., Eckert, E.D., and Davis, J.M. (1979).

Disturbances in body image estimation as related to other characteristics and outcome in anorexia nervosa. *British Journal of Psychiatry, 134*, 60-66.

Chen, S.H., and Bernard-Optic, V. (1993). Comparison of personal and computer-assisted instruction for children with autism. *Mental Retardation, 31*(6), 368-376.

Cioffi, G. (1993). Le variabili psicologiche implicate in un'esperienza virtuale (Psychological variables that influence a virtual experience). In G. Belotti (Ed.), *Del Virtuale (Virtuality)*. Milano: Il Rostro.

Cohen, D.C. (1977). Comparison of self-report and behavioral procedures for assessing acrophobia. *Behavior Therapy, 8*, 17-23.

Cohen, M. (1992). Integrating graphic and audio windows. *Presence: Teleoperators and Virtual Environments, 1*(4), 468-481.

Colby, K. M. (1968). Computer aided language development in non speaking children. *Arch. Gen. Psychiatry, 19*, 641-652.

Courchesne, E. (1989). Implications of recent neurobiological findings in autism. *Proceedings of the Conference of the Autism Society of America* (pp. 8-9). Washington, DC.

Cruz-Neira, Sandin, D.J., DeFanti, T.A., Kenyon, R.V., and Hart, J.C. (1992). The CAVE: Audio visual experience automatic virtual environment. *Communications of the ACM, 35*(6), 64-72.

Dasch, C.S. (1978). Relation of dance skills to body cathexis and locus of control orientation. *Perceptual and Motor Skills, 46*, 465-466.

Davis, C., and Cowles M. (1991). Body image and exercise: A study of relationships and comparisons between physically active men and women. *Sex Roles, 25*, 33-44.

Dede, C.J. (1992). The future of multimedia: Bridging to virtual words. *Educational Technology, 32*(5), 54-60.

Derogatis, C.R., Limpman, R.S., Rickels, K., Uhlenhuth, E.H., and Coul, L. (1974). The HSCL: A self-report inventory. *Behavioral Sciences 19*, 1-15.

DesLauriers, A.M., and Carlson, C.F. (1969). *Your child is asleep.* Homewood: The Dorsey Press.

Dixon (Ed.), (1992). *BMDP Statistical Software Manual to Accompany the 7.0 Software Release.* Berkeley, University of California Press.

Dolezal, H. (1982). *Living in a world transformed.* New York: Academic Press.

Durlach, N.I., Aviles, W.A., Pew, R.W., DiZio, P.A., and Zeltzer, D.L. (Eds.), (1992). *Virtual environment technology for training (VETT)*. (BBN Report No. 7661.). Cambridge, MA: Bolt Beranek and Newman, Inc.

Egan, D.E. (1988). Individual differences in human-computer interaction. In M. Helander (Ed.), *Handbook of Human-Computer Interaction* (pp. 543-556). North Holland, Amsterdam, Netherlands.

Ellis, A. (1962). *Reason and emotion in psychotherapy.* New York: Lyle Stuart.

Ellis, S.R., Kaiser, M., and Grunwald, A. (1991). *Pictorial communication in virtual and real environments*. London: Taylor & Francis.

Fisher, S. (1990). The evolution of psychological concepts about the body. In T.F. Cash, and T. Pruzinsky (Eds.), *Body images: Development, deviance and change*. New York: The Guilford Press.

Foe, E., and Wilson, R. (1991). *Stop obsessing: How to overcome your obsessions and compulsions*. New York: Bantam.

Fontaine, G. (1992). The experience of a sense of presence in intercultural and international encounters. *Presence: Teleoperators and Virtual Environments, 1*(4), 482.

Franklin, N., Tversky, B., and Coon, V. (1992). Switching points of view in spatial mental models. *Memory & Cognition, 20*(5), 507-518.

Freedman, R. (1990). Cognitive-behavioral perspectives on body-image change. In T.F. Cash, and T. Pruzinsky (Eds.), *Body images: Development, deviance and change*. New York: The Guilford Press.

Furness, T.A.(1993). Expeditions in virtual space. *Distinguished Lecture Series, Graphics, Visualization & Usability Center*, College of Computing, Georgia Institute of Technology.

Gallagher, S. (1995). Body schema and intentionality. In J.L. Bermstlgdez, A. Marcel, and N. Eilan. *The body and the self*. Cambridge, MA: MIT Press.

Gallagher, S. (1986). Body image and body schema: A conceptual clarification. *Journal of Mind & Behaviour, 4*, 541-554.

Garfinkel, P.E., and Garner, D.M. (1982). *Anorexia nervosa: a multidimensional perspective*. New York: Brunner & Mazel.

Garvey, W.P., and Hegrenes, J.R. (1966). Desensitization techniques in the treatment of school phobia. *American Journal of Orthopsychiatry, 36*, 147-52.

Gay, E.R. and Santiago, R. (1994). VR projects at natrona country, Wyoming. *Science - VR Applications bulletin.*

Goldberg, S. (1994) Training dismounted soldiers in a distributed interactive virtual environment. *U. S. Army Research Institute Newsletter, 14,* April, 9-12.

Grandin, T. (1992). An inside view of autism. In E. Schopler and G. B. Mesibov (Eds.), *High-functioning individuals with autism* (pp. 105-126). New York: Plenum Press.

Grandin, T., and Acariano, M. (1986). *Emergence: Labeled Autistic.* Novata, CA: Arena.

Gregory, R.L. (1991). Seeing by exploring. In S.R. Ellis (Ed.), *Pictorial communications in virtual and real environments* (pp. 328-337). London: Taylor and Francis.

Goisman, R.M., Warshaw, M.G., Steketee, G.S., Fierman, E.J., Rogers, M.P.,

Goldenberg, I., Weinshenker, N.J., Vasile, R.G., and Keller, M.B. (1995). DSM-IV and the disappearance of agoraphobia without a history of panic disorder: New data on a controversial diagnosis. *American Journal of Psychiatry, 152*(10), 1438-1443.

Hahn, J.K., Gritz, L., Darken, R. Geigel, J., and Won Lee, J. (1993). An integrated virtual environment system. *Presence: Teleoperators and Virtual Environments, 2*(4), 353-360.

Harris, C. S. (1965). Perceptual adaptation to inverted, reversed, and displaced vision. *Psychological Review, 72*, 419-444.

Haugland, S., and Shade, D. (1988). Developmentally appropriate software for young children, *Young Children, 43*, 37-43.

Head, H. (1926). *Aphasia and kindred disorders of speech.* London: Cambridge University Press.

Heeter, C. (1992). Being there: The subjective experience of presence. *Presence: Teleoperators and Virtual Environments, 1*(2), 262-71.

Heinich, R., Molenda, M., and Russell, J. (1993). Multimedia systems. *Instructional Media and the New Technologies of Instruction.* (pp. 271-273). New York: Macmillan.

Held, R.M., and Durlach, N.I. (1992). Presence. *Presence: Teleoperators and Virtual Environments 1*(1), 109-112.

Held, R.M. and Durlach, N.I. (1993). Telepresence, time delay, and adaptation. In S. Ellis (Ed.), *Pictorial communication in virtual and real environments* (pp. 232-246). Taylor and Francis, London.

Henry, D. and Fur, T. (1993). Spatial perception in virtual environments: Evaluating an architectural application. *Proceedings of the IEEE Virtual Reality Annual International Symposium.* Seattle, Washington.

Hergenhahn, B.R. (1988). *An Introduction to theories of learning (3rd ed.).* Englewood Cliffs: Prentice Hall.

Hettinger, L.J., Berbaum, K.S., Kennedy, R.S., Dunlap, W.P., and Nolan, M.D. (1990). Vection and simulator sickness. *Military Psychology, 2*(3), 171-181.

Hodges, L.F. (1992). Time-multiplexed stereoscopic computer graphics. *IEEE Computer Graphics and Applications, 12*(2), 20-30.

Hodges, L.F., Kooper, R., Meyer, T.C., Rothbaum, B.O., Opdyke, D., deGraaff, J.J., Williford, J.S., and North, M.M. (1995). Virtual environments for treating the fear of heights. *IEEE COMPUTER, Theme Feature,* July, 27-34.

Hodges, L.F., Rothbaum, B.A., Williford, J. S., Opdyke, D., Kooper, R., and North, M.M. (1994). Presence as the defining factor in a VR application. *SIGGRAPH '94.*

Howlett, E.M. (1990). Wide angle orthostereo. In J.O. Merritt, and S.S. Fisher

(Eds.), Stereoscopic displays and applications. *The International Society for Optical Engineering*. WA: Bellingham.

Hunsucker, G. (1988). *Attention deficit disorder*. Fort Worth, TX: Forresst Publishing.

James, J.E., Hampton, B.A., May T., and Larsen, S.A. (1983). The relative efficacy of imaginal and In Vivo desensitization in the treatment of agoraphobia. *Journal of Behavioral Therapy & Experimental Psychiatry,14,* 203-207.

Kallman, E.A. (1993). Ethical evaluation: A necessary element in virtual environment research. *Presence: Teleoperators and Virtual Environments, 2*(2), 143-146.

Kaplan, H.I., and Sadlock, B.J. (1990). *Pocket handbook of clinical psychiatry*. Baltimore: Williams and Wilkins.

Kalawsky, R.S. (1993). *The science of virtual reality and virtual environments*. New York: Addison-Wesley Publishing Co.

Kennedy, R.S., Lane, N.E., Lilienthal, M.G., Berbaum, K.S., and Hettinger, L.J. (1992). Profile analysis of simulator sickness symptoms: Application to virtual environment systems. *Presence: Teleoperators and Virtual Environments, 1,* 295-301.

Kennedy, R.S., Fowlkes, J.E., and Hettinger, L.J. (1989). *Review of Simulator Sickness Literature* (Tech Report NTSC TR89-024). Naval Training Systems Center, Orlando, FL.

Kijima, R., Shirakawa, K., Hirose, M., and Nihei, K. (1994). Virtual sand box: Development of an application of virtual environment for clinical medicine. *Presence: Teleoperators and Virtual Environments, 3(1),* 45-59.

Kozak, J.J., Hancock, P.A., Arthur, E.J., and Chrysler, S.T. (1993). Transfer of training from virtual reality. *Ergonomics, 36*(7), 777-784.

Kubovy, M. (1986). *The psychology of perspective and renaissance art*. Cambridge: Cambridge University Press.

Lampton, D.R., Knerr, B. W., Goldberg, S. L., Bliss, J.P., Moshell, J.M., and Blau, B.S. (1994). The virtual environment performance assessment battery (VEPAB): Development and evaluation. *Presence: Teleoperators and Virtual Environments, 3*(2), 145-157.

Lanier, J. (1992). Virtual reality: The promise of the future. *Interactive Learning*. 275-279.

Lang, P.J. (1977). Imagery in therapy: An information processing analysis of fear. *Behavior Therapy, 8,* 862-886.

Lang, P. J. (1979). A bioinformational theory of emotional imagery. *Psychophysiology, 16,* 495-512.

Larijani, L.C. (1994). *The virtual reality primer*. New York: McGraw-Hill.

Laurel, B. (1991). *Computer as theater*. New York: Addison-Wesley

Publishing Co.

Leuner, H. (1969). Guided affective imagery: A method of intensive psychotherapy. *American Journal of Psychotherapy, 23*, 4-21.

Loomis, J.M. (1993). Understanding synthetic experience must begin with the analysis of ordinary perceptual experience. *IEEE Symposium on Research Frontiers in Virtual Reality* (pp. 54-57). San Jose, California.

Loomis, J.M. (1992). Distal attribution and presence. *Presence: Teleoperators and Virtual Environments, 1*(1), 113-119.

Lovaas, O.I., Schreibman, L., Kroegel, R., and Rehm, R. (1977). Selective responding by autistic children to multiple sensory input. *Journal of Abnormal Psychology, 77*(3), 211-222.

Malone, T. W., and Lepper, M (1987). Making learning fun: A taxonomy of intrinsic motivations for Learning. In R.E. Snow and M.J. Farr (Eds.) Aptitude, learning, and instructions: III. *Cognitive and affective process analyses* (pp. 223 - 253). Hillsdale, NJ: Erlbaum

Marks, I.M., and Mathews, A.M. (1979). Brief standard self-rating for phobic patients. *Behavior Research and Therapy,* 17, 263-267.

Marshall, J. (1994). *Social phobia.* NY: Basic.

Massimino, M.J. and Sheridan, T.B. (1993). Sensory substitution for force feedback in teleoperation. *Presence: Teleoperators and Virtual Environments, 2*(4), 344-352.

McDowell, I. (1994). 3D Stereoscopic data for immersive displays. *AI Expert, 9*(5), 18-21.

McGovern, D.E. (1993). Experience and results in teleoperation of land vehicles. In S. Ellis (Ed.), *Pictorial communication in virtual and real environments* (pp. 182-195). Taylor and Francis, London.

Mesibov, G.B., Schopler, E., and Kearsey, K.A. (1994). Structured teaching. In E. Schopler and G.B. Mesibov (Eds.), *Behavioral issues in autism* (pp. 195-206). New York: Plenum Press.

Meyers, J.K., Weissman, M.M., Tischler, G.L., Holzer, C.E., Leaf, P.J., Orvaschel, H., Anthony, J., Boyd, J.H., Burke, J.D., Kraemer, M., and Stoltzman, R. (1984). Six month prevalence of psychiatric disorders in three communities: 1980-1982. *Archives of General Psychiatry, 41*, 959-967.

Michelson, L., Mavissakalian, M., and Marchione, K. (1985). Cognitive and behavioral treatment of agrophobia: Clinical, behavioral, and psychophysiological outcomes. *Journal of Consulting and Clinical Psychology 53*, 913-925.

Middleton, T. (Ed.), (1992). *Virtual worlds: Real challenges.* Westport: Meckler Publishing.

Middleton, T., and Boman, D. (1994). Simon says: Using speech to perform tasks in virtual environments. *The Second Annual Conference on Virtual Reality and Persons with Disabilities*. San Francisco.

MMVR-IV (1996). *Proceedings of the Medicine Meets Virtual Reality IV Conference*, (pp. 713-730), San Diego, CA.

Moshell, J.M, and Hughes, C.E. (1994). Shared virtual worlds for education. *Virtual Reality World, 2*(1), 63-74.

Moshell, J.M., Blau, B.S., Knerr, B., Lampton, D.R., and Bliss, J. P. (1993). A research testbed for virtual environment training applications. *Proceedings of the IEEE Virtual Reality Annual International Symposium* (pp. 83-89). Seattle, Washington.

Mowafy, L., Russo, T., and Miller, L. (1993). Is "presence" a training issue? *IEEE Symposium on Research Frontiers in Virtual Reality* (pp. 124-125). San Jose, California.

Naiman, A. (1992). Presence, and other gifts. *Presence: Teleoperators and Virtual Environments, 1*(1), 145-148.

Newquist, H.P. (1992). Virtual reality's commercial reality. *Computer World*.

North, S.M. (1996). Effectiveness of Virtual Reality in the Motivational Processes of Learners. *International Journal of Virtual Reality, 2*(1), 17-21.

North, S.M. (1996). The effect of the virtual reality on improving learner's intrinsic motivation and interests. *Electronic Journal of Virtual Culture*, Winter issue.

North, M.M., North, S.M., and Coble, J.R. (1997). Virtual environment psychotherapy: A case study of fear of flying disorder. *Presence: Teleoperators and Virtual Environments. 6*(1), (in press).

North, M.M., North, S.M., and Coble, J.R. (1996c). Effectiveness of virtual environment desensitization in the treatment of agoraphobia. *Presence: Teleoperators and Virtual Environments. 5*(4), (in press).

North, M.M., and North, S.M. (1996b). Virtual psychotherapy. *Journal of Medicine and Virtual Reality, 1*(2), 28-32.

North, M.M., North, S.M., and Coble, J.R.(1996a). Application: Psychotherapy, Flight Fear Flees, *CyberEdge Journal, 6*(1), 8-10.

North, M.M., North, S.M., and Coble, J.R. (1995b). Effectiveness of virtual environment desensitization in the treatment of agoraphobia. *International Journal of Virtual Reality, 1*(2), 25-34.

North, M.M., North, S.M., and Coble, J.R. (1995a). An effective treatment for psychological disorders: Treating agoraphobia with virtual environment desensitization. *CyberEdge Journal, 5*(3), 12-13.

North, M.M., and North, S.M. (1994). Virtual environments and psychological disorders. *Electronic Journal of Virtual Culture, 2*(4), 37-42(ep.).

Oren, T. (1990). Designing a new medium. In B. Laurel (Ed.), *The art of human-computer interface design* (pp. 467-479). Addison-Wesley

Publishing Co.

Orintz, E. (1985). Neurophysiology of infantile autism. *Journal of the American Academy of Child Psychiatry, 24*, 251-262.

Pantelidis, V.S. (1993). Virtual reality in the classroom. *Educational Technology, 33*(4), 23-27.

Panyan, M.V. (1984). Computer technology for autistic students. *Journal of Autistic and Developmental Disorders, 14*(4), 375-382.

Park, D., and Youderian, P. (1974). Light and number: Ordering principles in the world of an autistic child. *Journal of Autism and Childhood Schizophrenia, 4*, 313-323.

Patterson, Cecil H. (1986). *Theories of counseling and psychotherapy.* New York: Harper & Row.

Pausch, R., Shackelford, M.A., and Proffitt, D. (1993). A user study comparing head-mounted and stationary displays. *Proceedings of the IEEE Symposium on Research Frontiers in Virtual Reality* (pp. 41-45). San Jose, California.

Pausch, R., Crea, T., and Conway, M. (1992). A literature survey for virtual environments: Military flight simulator visual systems and simulator sickness. *Presence: Teleoperators and Virtual Environments, 1*(3), 344.

Pendleton, M.G., and Higgins, R.L. (1983). A comparison of negative practice and systematic desensitization in the treatment of acrophobia. *Journal of Behavioral Therapy and Experimental Psychiatry, 14*(4), 317-323.

Pimentel and Teixeira (1992). Through the looking glass. *Intel / Blue Ridge Summit*, PA: Windcrest/McGraw-Hill.

Plienis, A.J., and Romanczyk, R.G. (1985). Analysis of performance, behavior, and predictors for severely disturbed children: A comparison of adult vs. computer instruction. *Analysis and Intervention in Developmental Disabilities, 5*(4), 345-356.

Psotka, J., Davison, S.A., and Lewis, S.A. (1993). Exploring immersion in virtual space. *Virtual Reality Systems, 1*(2), 70-92.

Psotka, J., and Davison, S.A. (1993). Cognitive Factors Associated with Immersion in Virtual Environments. *Proceedings of the Conference on Intelligent Computer-Aided Training and Virtual Environment Technology.* Houston, TX.

Psotka, J., and Lewis, A. (1994). Effects of field of view on judgements of self-location. (in preparation).

Psotka, J., and Calvert, S. (1994). Measuring heart rate reduces the experiences of immersion in VR. (in preparation).

Ray T. C., King L.J., and Grandin T. (1988). The effectiveness of self-initiated vestibular stimulation in producing speech sounds in an autistic child. *Journal of Occupational Therapy and Research, 8*, 186-190.

Regian, J.W., Shebilske, W., and Monk, J. (1993). VR as a *training tool:*

Transfer effects. Unpublished manuscript. Armstrong Laboratory, Brooks Air Force Base, Texas.

Regian, J.W., Shebilske, W., and Monk, J. (1992). A preliminary empirical evaluation of virtual reality as an instructional medium for visual-spatial tasks. *Journal of Communications, 42*(4), 136-149.

Reyker, J. (1977). Spontaneous visual imagery: Implications for psycho-analysis, psychopathology and psychotherapy. *Journal of Mental Imagery, 2,* 253-274.

Ritvo, E.R., and Freeman, B.J. (1978). National society for autistic children definition of the syndrome of autism. *Journal of the American Academy of Child Psychiatry, 17,* 565-576.

Roll, J.P., and Roll, R. (1988). From eye to foot: A proprioceptive chain involved in postural control. In G. Amblard, A. Berthoz, and F. Clarac (Eds.), *Posture and gait: Development, adaptation, and modulation.* Amsterdam: Excerpta Medica.

Rosen, J.C. (1990). Body image disturbances in Eating Disorders. In T.F. Cash, and T. Pruzinsky (Eds.), *Body Images: Development, Deviance and Change.* The Guilford Press: New York.

Rossi, A.M., and Seiler, W. J. (1990). The comparative effectiveness of systematic desensitization and an integrative approach in treating public speaking anxiety: A literature review and a preliminary investigation. Imagination, *Cognition and Personality, 9*(1), 49-66.

Rothbaum, B.O., Hodges, L.F., Opdyke, D., Kooper, R., Williford, J.S., and North, M.M. (1995b). Virtual reality graded exposure in the treatment of acrophobia: A case study. *Journal of Behavior Therapy, 26*(3), 547-554.

Rothbaum, B., Hodges, L., Kooper, R., Opdyke, D., Williford, J., and North, M. (1995a). Effectiveness of computer-generated (virtual reality) graded exposure in the treatment of acrophobia. *American Journal of Psychiatry, 152*(4), 626-628.

Ruggieri, V., Milizia, M., Sabatini, N., and Tosi, M.T. (1983). Body perception in relation to muscular tone at rest and tactile sensitivity to tickle. *Perceptual and Motor Skills.*

Russell, M.C. (1992). *Towards a neuropsychological approach to PTSD: An integrative conceptualization of etiology and mechanisms of therapeutic change.* Unpublished doctoral dissertation, Pacific Graduate School of Psychology, Palo Alto, CA.

Rutter, M. (1978). Diagnosis and definition of childhood Autism. *Journal of Autistic and Childhood Schizophrenia, 8,* 1938-1961.

Sabatini, N., Ruggieri, V., and Milizia, M. (1984). Barrier and penetration scores in relation to some objective and subjective somesthetic measures. *Perceptual and Motor Skills, 59,* 195-202.

Sadowsky, J., and Massof, R.W. (1994). Sensory engineering: The science of synthetic environments. *John Hopkins APL Technical Digest, 15*, 99-109.

Salamon, G., Perkins, D.N., and Globerson, T. (1991). Partners in cognition: Extending human intelligence with intelligent technologies. *Educational Researcher, 20*(3), 2-9.

Sawyer, W.D. (1992). The virtual computer: A new paradigm for educational computing. *Educational Technology.* 7-14.

Schetz, K.F. (1994). Teacher-assisted computer implementation. *A Vygotskian perspective, Early Education and Review, 5*(1), 18-26.

Schilder, P. (1950). *The image and appearance of the human body.* New York: International Universities Press.

Schlager, M.S., Boman, D., Piantanida, T, and Stephenson R. (1992). Fore casting the impact of virtual environment technology on maintenance training. *The Space Operations, Applications, and Research Symposium.* Houston, TX: NASA JSC.

Schneider, J. W. (1982). Lens-assisted in vivo desensitization to heights. *Journal of Behavior Therapy & Experimental Psychiatry 13*(4), 333-336.

Schopler, E. (1987). Specific and nonspecific treatment factors in the effectiveness of a treatment system. *American Psychologist, 42*, 379-383.

Sellen, A., and Nicol, A. (1990). Building user-centered on-line help. In B. Laurel (Ed.), *The art of human-computer interface design* (pp. 143-153). MA: Addison-Wesley Publishing Co.

Shapiro, F. (1995). *Eye movement desensitization and reporocessing.* New York: The Guilford Press.

Sheridan, T.B. (1992). Musings on telepresence and virtual presence. *Presence: Teleoperators and Virtual Environments, 1*(1), 120-126.

Sheridan,T.B. (1993). My anxieties about virtual environments. *Presence: Teleoperators and Virtual Environments, 2*(2), 141-142.

Shneiderman, B. (1992). *Designing the user interface.* MA: Addison-Wesley.

Sinclair, J. (1992). Bridging the gaps: An inside-out view of autism (or, do you know what I don't know?). In E. Schopler and G. B. Mesibov (Eds.), *High-functioning individuals with autism* (pp. 294-302). New York: Plenum Press.

Skinner, B.F. (1971). Beyond freedom and dignity, New York: Knopf.

Skrinar, G.S., Bullen, B.A., Cheek, J.M., McArthur, J.W., and Vaughan, L.K. (1986). Effects of endurance training on body-consciousness in women. *Perceptual and Motor Skills, 62,* 483-490.

Slater, M. and Usoh, M. (1993). The influence of a virtual body on presence in immersive virtual environments. *Proceedings of the Third Annual Conference on Virtual Reality* (pp. 34-42). Westport, CT: Meckler Ltd.

Sollenberger, R.L., and Milgram, P. (1993). Effects of stereoscopic and rotational displays in a three-dimensional path tracing task. *Human Factors, 35*(3), 483-499.

Steuer, J. (1992). Defining virtual reality: Dimensions determining telepresence. *Journal of Communication, 42*, 73-93.

Stone, V.E. (1993). Social interaction and social development in virtual environments. *Presence: Teleoperators and Virtual Environments 2*(2), 153-161.

Strickland, D., Marcus, L., Hogan, K., Mesibov, G., and McAllister, D. (1995). Using virtual reality as a learning aid for autistic children. *Proceedings of the Autism France 3rd International Conference on Computers and Autism* (pp. 119-132). Nice, France.

Stunkard, A., and Burt, V. (1967). Obesity and the body game: II. Age of onset of disturbances in body image. *American Journal of Psychiatry, 123*, 1447-1447.

Stunkard, A., and Mendelson, M. (1961). Disturbances in body image of some obese persons, *American Journal of Dietology, 38*, 57-63.

Sutherland, I. (1965). The ultimate display. *Proceedings of IFIP 65(2)*, 506-8.

Teitel, M. A. (1990). The eyephone: A head-mounted stereo display. *Proceedings of SPIE, 1256,* 168-171.

Thomas, J. C., and Stuart, R. (1992). Virtual reality and human factors. *Proceedings of the Human Factors Society 36th Annual Meeting* (pp. 207-210). Atlanta, GA.

Thompson, J.K. (1992). Body Image: Extent of disturbance, associated features, theoretical models, assessment methodologies, intervention strategies, and a proposal for a new DSM IV diagnostic category - Body Image Disorder. In M. Hersa, R.M. Eisler, and P.M. Miller (Eds.), *Progress in behavior modification.* Sycamore (IL): Sicamore.

Thompson, J.K. (1990). *Body image disturbance: Assessment and Treatment.* Elmsford, NJ: Pergamon Press.

Thompson, J.K., and Altabe, M.N. (1991). Psychometric qualities of the figure rating scale. *International Journal of Eating Disorders, 10*, 615-619.

Thompson, J.K., Berland, N.W., Linton, P.H., and Weinsier, R. (1986). Assessment of body distortion via a self-adjusting light beam in seven eating disorders groups. *International Journal of Eating Disorders, 7*, 113-120.

Thompson, M.A, and Gray, J.J. (1995). Development and validation of a new body-image assessment scale. *Journal of Personality Assessment, 2*, 258-269.

Thompson, J.K. (1995). Assessment of body image. In D.B. Allison (Ed.), *Handbook of assessment methods for eating behaviors and weight related problems.* Thousand Oaks, CA: Sage.

Thyer, B.A., Papsdorf, J.D., Davis, R., and Vallecorsa, S. (1984). Autonomic correlates of the subjective anxiety scale. *Journal of Behavior Therapy and Experimental Psychiatry, 15*, 3-7.

Tsai, L.Y. (1992). Diagnostic issues in high-functioning autism. In E.Schopler and G.B. Mesibov (Eds.), *High-functioning individuals with autism* (pp. 11-40). New York: Plenum Press.

Valtolina, G., Molinari, E., Borgomainerio, E., and Riva, G. (1994). Body size estimation in anorexia nervosa. *Advancements in Diagnosis and Treatment of Anorexia and Obesity.* Rome: SIS.DCA.

Vandereycken, W., Probst, M., and Meermann, R. (1988). An experimental video-confrontation procedure as a therapeutic technique and a research tool in the treatment of eating disorders. In K.M. Pirke, W. Vandereycken, and D. Ploog (Eds.), *The psychobiology of bulimia nervosa.* Heidelberg: Springer-Verlag.

Varner, D. (1993). Olfaction and VR. *Proceedings of the Conference on Intelligent Computer-Aided Training and Virtual Environment Technology,* Houston, TX.

Viirre, E. (1994). A survey of medical issues and virtual reality technology. *Virtual Reality World,* 16-20.

Ware, C., Kevin W. A., and Kellogg S.B. (1993). Fish tank virtual reality. *Proceedings of INTERCHI '93 Conference on Human Factors in Computing Systems* (pp. 149-160). Amsterdam.

Warner, H.D., Serfoss, G.L., and Hubbard, D.C. (1993). Effects of area of interest display characteristics on visual search performance and head movements in simulated low level flight. *Armstrong Laboratory Technical Report #0023.*

Watson, J.B., and Rayner, R. (1920). Conditioned emotional reactions. *Journal of Experimental Psychology, 3*, 1-14.

Weissman, M.M. (1985). The epidemiology of anxiety disorders: Rates, risks and familial patterns. In A.H. Tuma and J.D. Maser (Eds.), *Anxiety and the anxiety disorders.* Hillside, NJ: Erlbaum.

Wertheim, A.H., and Mesland, B. (1993). Motion perception during linear ego-motion. *Institute for Perception Technical Report IZF-1993-3,* TNO Institute for Perception, Soesterberg, The Netherlands.

Wexelblat, A.(Ed.), (1993). *Virtual reality applications and explorations.* Toronto: Academic Press Professional.

Whiteback, C. (1993). Virtual environments: Ethical issues and significant confusions. *Presence: Teleoperators and Virtual Environments, 2*(2),147-152.

Wickens, C.D., Merwin, D.H., and Lin, E.L. (1994). Implications of graphics enhancements for the visualization of scientific data: dimensional integrality, stereopsis, motion, and mesh. *Human Factors, 36*(1), 44-61.

Williams S.L., Dooseman, G., and Kleinfield, E. (1984). Comparative effectiveness of guided mastery and exposure treatments for intractable phobias. *Journal of Consulting and Clinical Psychology, 52*, 505-518.

Williford, J.S., Hodges, L.F., North, M.M., and North, S.M. (1993). Relative effectiveness of virtual environment desensitization and imaginal desensitization in the treatment of acrophobia. *Proceedings of Graphics Interface '93 Conference.* 162.

Wing, L. (1972). *Autistic children, a guide for parents and professionals.* New York: Brunner/Mazel.

Wolpe, J. (1982). *The practice of behavior therapy (3rd ed.).* New York: Pergamon.

Wolpe, J. (1961). The systematic desensitization of neuroses. *Journal of Neuroses and Mental Diseases 132,* 189-203.

Wolpe, J. (1958). *Psychotherapy for reciprocal inhibition.* Palo Alto, CA: Stanford University Press.

Wolpert, L. (1990). Field-of-view information for self-motion perception. In R. Warren, and A.H. Wertheim (Eds.), *Perception and control of self-motion* (pp.101-126). Lawrence Erlbaum, Hillsdale, NJ: Lawrence Erlbaum.

Wooley, S.C., and Wooley, O.W. (1985). Intensive out-patient and residential treatment for bulimia. In Garner, D. M., and Garfinkel, P. E. (Eds.), *Handbook of psychotherapy for anorexia and bulimia.* New York: Guilford Press.

Zeltzer, D. (1992). Autonomy, interaction and presence. *Presence:Tele-operators and Virtual Environments, 1*(1), 127-132.

INDEX

❖ ❖ ❖

About the Authors

Max M. North, Ph.D. is a tenured Assistant Professor in the Computer Information Science Department and Director of the Human-Computer Interaction Group and Virtual Reality Technology Laboratory at Clark Atlanta University. He is the author of many articles in the field of computing and psychology and the recipient of an award from Sigma Xi, the Scientific Research Society. Dr. North's major contribution to the scientific community is his discovery and continuous strong research activities in the innovative area of virtual reality therapy which has received international attention and coverage in the scientific community and the popular media, including the *New York Times, U.S. News and World Report, PBS, NBC, ABC, etc.*

Contact Information: 1-404-880-6942, Max@acm.org

Sarah M. North, M.S.D. is an Assistant Professor in the Computer and Information Science Department at Clark Atlanta University. She is Co-Director of the Human-Computer Interaction Group and Virtual Reality Technology Laboratory. She is the author of several articles in the field of computing and psychology. Professor North's field of research is cognitive science and human-computer interaction. Essentially her work emphasizes the effectiveness of virtual reality in the motivational processes of learners. Her research activities have been reported in several media (e.g., *Atlanta Computer Currents, U.S. News and World Report*, etc.).

Contact Information: 1-404-880-6957, Sarah@acm.org

Joseph R. Coble, Ph.D. is a tenured Professor in the Psychology Department at Clark Atlanta University. He has been one of the most active members of the Human-Computer Interaction and Virtual Reality Technology Laboratory research team. He has published several papers in the field of psychology and computing. Dr. Coble's research activities in collaboration with Dr. North and Prof. North have been reported by several media. Dr.Coble received his training as a research psychologist from the Psychobiology program at Florida State University with a masters in human vision and a doctorate in behavioral genetics.

Contact Information: 1-404-880-8259, jrcoble@prodigy.com